THE GREAT
CHICKEN
COOKBOOK

Introduced by Judith Ferguson
Photography by Peter Barry
Designed by Claire Leighton, Jill Coote, and Richard Hawke
Edited by Kate Cranshaw and Jillian Stewart
Typesetting by Julie Smith

Recipes on pages 28, 32, 36, 42, 44, 48, 50, 52, 54, 60, 62, 92, 94, 114, 124, 126, 128, 130,134, 138, 142, 158, 160, 164, 166 and 172, courtesy of The British Chicken Information Service

CLB 3255
© 1993 Colour Library Books Ltd., Godalming, Surrey.
All rights reserved.
Printed and bound by Tien Wah Press, Singapore.
ISBN 1-85833-044-0

THE GREAT
CHICKEN
COOKBOOK

JUDITH FERGUSON

Colour Library Books

CONTENTS

$\mathcal{I}$NTRODUCTION

Down through the ages, politicians on both sides of the Atlantic have been promising a chicken in every pot. That's because chicken has always been a symbol of prosperity. Most countries in the world have a classic chicken dish in their culinary repertoire. In France it's Coq au Vin, in the USA it's Southern Fried Chicken, Hungary has Chicken Paprika and England has its roast chicken with all the trimmings. In China and India the variations are too numerous to name just one.

Before the days of intensive farming, chickens were a once-a-week treat on Sunday, but as they became more readily available, problems developed. Chickens began to lose their flavour, and health hazards, due to the very techniques that made chicken more available, made people wary of eating them. This was a blessing in disguise, because it led the poultry industry to explore new ways of rearing chickens. As a result many birds were better fed and cared for and the public was rewarded with birds with a much better flavour.

With the advent of new rearing ideas came Corn-fed and Free-range chickens. Corn-fed chickens have a golden colour which is due to their feed, but they aren't necessarily free-range. Free-range chickens often have their diets supplemented with corn, so they, too, will have the same golden colour.

The EEC has set up a three tier system for definition: Traditional Free-range birds are old fashioned slow-growing breeds reared with a minimum of 39 days of continuous day time outdoor access over an 81 day period; Free-range birds are modern fast-growing breeds more densely reared and have a minimum of 28 days continuous outdoor access over a 56 day period; Free-range Total Freedom birds are breeds that naturally range for their food and must be reared in open air runs of unlimited area from a maximum of six weeks old. All three types must have feed containing at least 70 per cent cereals. Free-range chickens are more expensive, but worth the price for their superior flavour and more humane treatment.

There are other distinctions among chickens, too, as you will see, but whatever the description, chicken can be the basis for so many different, delicious and nutritious recipe ideas that you will never be lost for inspiration.

Choosing Chicken

Poussin is the French name for young or "spring" chicken. Single poussins usually weigh about 400g/14oz and serve one person; double poussins, weighing between 560-675g/1¼-1½lbs, usually feed two people.

Types and cuts of chicken

Clockwise from top left: Oak smoked chicken, corn fed chicken, roasting chicken, chicken quarter, skinned chicken breast, chicken wing, chicken drumstick, chicken breast with skin, poussin, spatchcocked chicken.

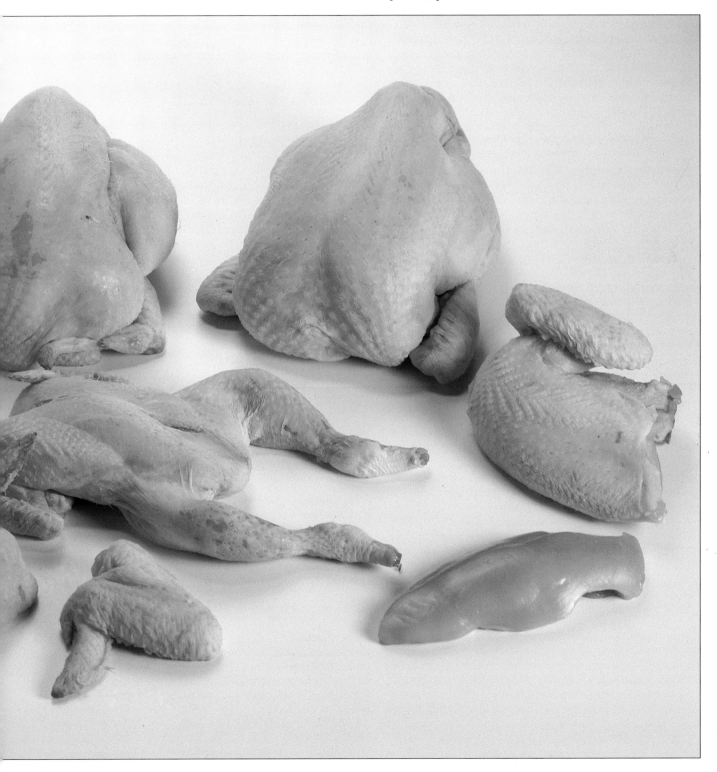

Both can be fried, grilled or sautéed, and are often boned and stuffed or spachcocked (split and flattened out).

Broilers or roasting chickens, can weigh anything between 900g-2.7kg/2-6lbs, the average being about 1.4-2kg/3-4½lbs; and besides roasting, other cooking methods – such as frying, baking, or casseroling – work equally well.

A capon is a neutered young rooster. This process can be carried out by a small operation or by implanting hormones into the bird's neck. Although the production of capons is not allowed in Britain, they can be imported and sold her but only on the condition that there are no hormone residues in the meat. Capons are raised to be very plump, and can weight up to 8lb/3.6kg. These are best roasted or casseroled to make the most of their rich and distinctive flavour.

Boiling or stewing chickens were once abundant but are now seldom seen. These are older and tougher birds which need long, moist cooking and make delicious soups. A male chicken too old to roast is called a cock. A fowl is a hen of the same age.

Buying Chicken

You can buy chicken in many different forms – split in half, in quarters, portioned into thighs, drumsticks, wings or breasts. Breasts come bone-in, part-boned or completely boned, with the skin on or off. Boned and skinned chicken breasts, which include the top bone of the wing, are called suprêmes. Chicken comes diced, minced, cut in strips for stir-frying or threaded on skewers. You can choose from stuffed breasts, thighs or a whole stuffed bird ready for roasting. You will find chicken portions marinated, or in sauces ready to cook.

Chicken wrapped for the supermarket cabinet will be labelled with the date that it should be sold by and the date that you should eat it by. Even through the wrapping, you can tell if a bird has bruised or otherwise damaged skin, by discoloured patches or the skin looking shrivelled and dry – all signs of a substandard bird. Where colour is concerned, remember that battery-farmed chickens will look very pale compared to corn-fed or free-range ones. On chicken pieces, the flesh next to the bone is normally slightly darker. Most of the cuts that are available fresh, are also available frozen.

Storing Fresh and Frozen Chicken

If you can't take the chicken straight home from the supermarket or if the weather is very warm, take a insulated bag along with you when you shop. Put the chicken immediately into the refrigerator when you get it home, but not right next to cooked food or on the shelf above. Place chicken in its wrapper on a plate large enough to contain any drips.

Don't freeze uncooked chicken unless you are certain it hasn't been frozen before. Never freeze chicken that isn't absolutely fresh. Any bacteria will just lie dormant while the chicken is frozen and will start multiplying as soon as the chicken starts to thaw. If you buy it ready frozen, put it into your home freezer as soon as possible in its original wrapping. Freeze uncooked chicken for up to three months and cooked for up to two months, but check your own freezer's instructions.

Whenever possible, thaw the chicken in the refrigerator or at least in a cool room. Make sure it is completely defrosted before cooking. There should be no ice crystals in the cavity and the legs should be soft and flexible. There is really no nutritional difference between fresh and frozen chicken, providing it hasn't been frozen longer than the recommended time.

Nutritious Chicken

Chicken is a favourite with calorie and health conscious people for several very good reasons. It's low in fat, and contains a high proportion of unsaturated fatty acids, which is very important in low cholesterol diets. Although the skin contains the most calories, even with it, 100g/3½oz of chicken is just 230 calories. Ounce for ounce chicken has more protein than red meat, and contains useful amounts of thiamine, riboflavin and nicotinic acid from the Vitamin B complex. The fact that it can be cooked so many different ways helps make low fat or low calorie diets more satisfying, too.

Preparing Chicken

There are a few commonsense rules to follow when preparing chicken:

Wash your hands thoroughly in hot, soapy water and rinse well.

Remove the chicken from the refrigerator just before you want to prepare it so that it doesn't stand too long at room temperature.

Place chicken on a clean chopping board. Use one board for raw meat and poultry only. Plastic boards are more hygienic than wood as they can be more thoroughly cleaned after use.

Rinse chicken after jointing or before cooking it whole and pat dry on kitchen paper.

Cooking Chicken

Oven roasting
Cook a 3½lb/1.6kg chicken for 20 minutes per 460g/1lb plus 20 minutes more at 190°C/375°F/Gas Mark 5. Cook larger chickens and capons – 170°C/325°F/Gas Mark 3 for about 25 minutes per 460g/1lb, plus 25 minutes more.

For fast roasting set the oven to 200°C/400°F/Gas Mark 6, cover chicken completely with foil and roast 20 minutes per 460g/1lb and 20 minutes more. Remove foil 20 minutes before the end of cooking time.

To test, stick a skewer into the thickest part of the thigh, if the juices run clear, the chicken is done.

Cook boned, stuffed chickens at 180°C/350°F/Gas Mark 4 for 30 minutes per 460g/1lb, covered loosely. Test with a meat thermometer, in the centre of the bird – it should read 75°C/170°F. Leave to stand for 10 minutes before removing stitches and carving.

Poaching

Rub the surface of a whole chicken with lemon juice and place in a large pan with a bouquet garni (parsley stalk, bay leaf and sprig of thyme), a peeled carrot, a stick of celery, an onion stuck with a clove, and enough water to cover. Bring to the boil and skim any scum from the surface as it rises. Simmer gently until tender, about 2-3 hours. Cook uncovered for a clearer cooking liquid.

Strain and reserve the liquid. Leave to stand until the fat rises to the surface, then skim off or refrigerate overnight. The fat will solidify, and can then be easily lifted off the top of the liquid.

Chicken breasts can be poached in a frying pan with stock and wine to cover, and seasoned with herbs. Simmer for 15-20 minutes or until tender.

Stock making

Place raw or cooked bones in a large pan and cover with water. Add a bouquet garni, chopped onion, carrot, celery, and a few black peppercorns. Add onion skin too, for a richer looking stock. Seeded tomatoes can be added and so can any root vegetable. Add giblets, if wished, but not the liver as this will make the stock bitter.

Bring to the boil, skimming off any scum that surfaces. Simmer for 2-3 hours, skimming occasionally. Strain and remove the fat in the same way as for poached chicken.

Stuffing a chicken

1 Lift the neck flap and loosen the skin from the flesh around the wishbone.

2 Place the stuffing under the neck flap, pushing in as much as you can without stretching the skin too much.

3 Pull the neck flap back over the stuffing, shaping it until nicely rounded and plump. Tuck the ends under the wing tips and secure with a skewer.

An alternative way of stuffing is to loosen all the skin over the breast and push the stuffing in between the flesh and the skin to evenly cover the whole breast.

Trussing a chicken

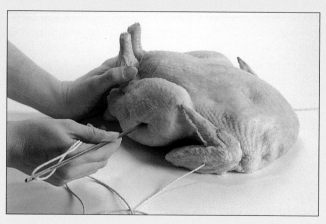

1 *Place chicken breast side up, pass the trussing needle (threaded with twine) through one wing joint, leaving about 7.5cm/3 inches of string protruding from the wing, through the body of the chicken and out through the wing on the opposite side.*

2 *Now push the needle through the skin just under the drumstick joint, through the body to come out in the same position on the opposite side.*

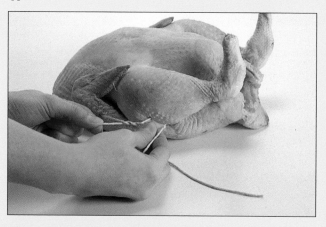

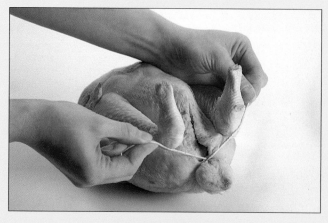

3 *Remove the needle and securely tie the two ends of twine together.*

4 *Pass a piece of string under the parsons nose, cross the string over and bring one end under each leg.*

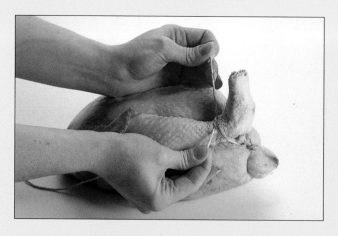

5 *Cross the ends over, back up across the legs and tie securely.*

Jointing

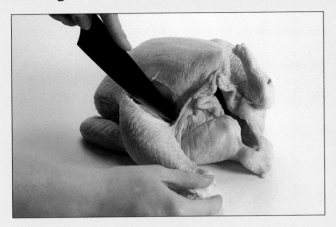

1 Cut through the chicken at the point where each leg joins the body.

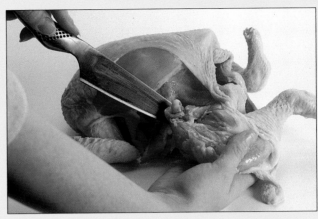

2 Bend each leg outwards to break the ball and socket joint. Use the tip of a sharp knife to separate the oyster (succulent eye of meat) from underneath the body to totally detach each leg.

3 Turn the chicken upside down and using a sharp heavy knife or a pair of poultry shears, cut through both sides of the rib cage just underneath the breast meat and the wing joints.

4 Turn the chicken back over and cut all the way along the breast bone to divide it into two pieces.

5 Cut each breast piece into two, leaving a portion of white meat attached to the wing joints.

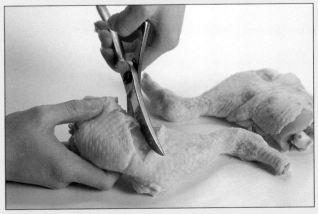

6 Bend the leg pieces back and forth to find the joint between the drumstick and thigh and cut between the two to separate them.

Boning a whole chicken

1 *Place the chicken breast side down on a chopping board, and using a sharp knife, cut through the skin along the backbone right down to the bone. Remove the parsons nose.*

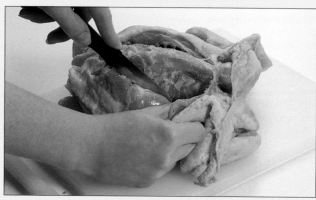

2 *Using the tip of a small sharp knife, scrape against the bone down the length of the cut you have made to begin lifting the skin and flesh away from the bone. Ensure you do not cut through the skin and always angle the knife into the bone.*

3 *Work the knife in the same way all the way down around the rib cage to the wing joints and leg joints.*

4 *Use the point of the knife to cut between the ball and socket joint of the leg. Sever the sinews to separate the legs from the body. Cut through the wing joints on both sides and sever the sinews.*

5 *Continue cutting against the bones around the rib cage until you reach the breast bone. Cut around the wishbone and remove it.*

6 *Starting at the neck end, cut close to the breast bone towards the tail end to remove the carcass. Lift the carcass as you cut, being careful not to nick the breast skin.*

Flattening and filling chicken breasts

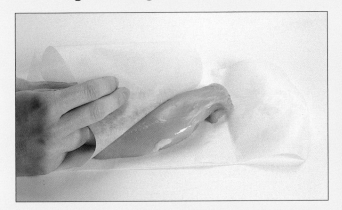

1 *Place the skinned chicken breast between two sheets of dampened greaseproof or waxed paper.*

2 *Use a rolling pin or meat mallet to flatten the chicken by beating it evenly from the middle out to the ends until it is about 7.5mm/⅓ inch thick.*

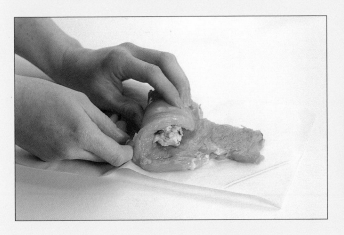

3 *Place filling on one end and fold in the sides to enclose. Roll up like a Swiss roll and secure with a cocktail stick.*

4 *Dust lightly with flour, brush with beaten egg and then roll in breadcrumbs. Deep-fry, shallow fry or bake.*

Stuffing chicken breasts

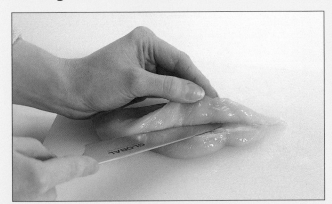

1 *On the thick side of the breast, cut a pocket along the side about 0.5-1.25cm/¼-½ inch from either end.*

2 *Fill with stuffing and reshape, securing the cut side with a skewer or cocktail stick.*

Braising, casseroling and sautéing

To braise, lightly brown a whole chicken or portions in a little oil or butter, then remove and fry the chopped vegetables. Replace chicken on top, cover and cook at 160°C/325°F/Gas Mark 3 until tender.

To casserole, coat chicken portions lightly in flour, then fry until golden. Add stock and wine to come nearly halfway up the chicken. Add chopped herbs, salt and pepper. Cover and cook for about 1 hour as for braising. Add lightly cooked vegetables halfway through cooking.

To sauté, brown chicken portions or halved poussins skin side down in hot oil or butter. Pour off most of the oil and add the sauce ingredients to the pan. Cover and cook on top of the stove until tender (about 30-40 minutes including browning time).

Stir-frying

For stir-frying, slice the chicken when it is very cold as this makes it easier to handle and allows thinner, more even strips to be cut. Use skinned and boned breasts or thigh meat and cut the meat into diagonal strips across the grain (this keeps the meat tender as it cooks), or into large dice.

Cook strips of chicken in a little oil in a wok or frying pan over high heat. Keep the chicken moving as it cooks by tossing it with a spatula or large spoon. When almost cooked, add the other ingredients. Be sure to have everything prepared before starting to cook.

Grilling and frying

Use a spatchcocked bird or portions, small chickens or poussins are the best size for this method of preparation.

Place the chicken breast side down on a chopping board and using poultry shears, cut down both sides of the back bone to remove it.

Turn the bird over and press down very firmly on the breast bone with the heal of your hand until it cracks and the bird flattens out. Turn the drumsticks inwards and trim off the wing tips.

To make the bird easier to handle whilst cooking, and to help hold its shape, thread two long skewers diagonally through the bird from legs to opposite wings.

Marinate first or just brush with oil and seasonings. Pre-heat the grill and cook about 10-15 minutes per side about 10cm/4in away from the heat.

For outdoor barbecuing, start grilling about 15cm/6in away from the coals, then move closer, or pre-cook chicken and then finish on the grill.

For frying, coat chicken portions in flour or with flour, then egg and finish with breadcrumbs. For shallow frying, brown portions quickly in hot oil, then lower the heat and fry gently until the meat is tender – about 15-20 minutes. For deep-frying, choose portions from a small chicken. Heat the oil to 190°C/375°F and cook portions for 10-15 minutes, turning frequently. Do not pierce the chicken when frying.

For goujons, cut skinned and boned chicken breasts

Roasting chicken

1 *Place the chicken in a roasting tin and cover with foil.*

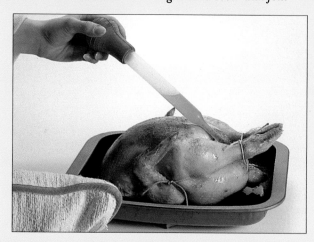

2 *Baste the chicken with the juices from the tin using a 'bulb' baster.*

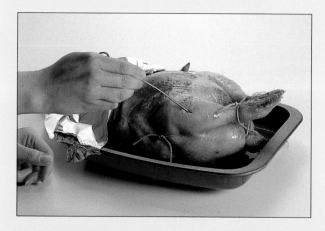

3 *To test if the chicken is cooked, insert a skewer into the thickest part of the leg. If the juices run clear the chicken is cooked, if the juices are pink then return the chicken to the oven for a further ten minutes before testing again.*

Carving a cooked chicken

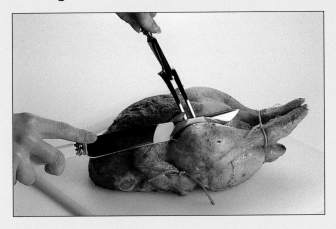

1 *Holding the chicken steady with a long pronged fork, cut down between the leg and body.*

2 *Break the joint by pressing one way with the carving knife and the opposite direction with the fork.*

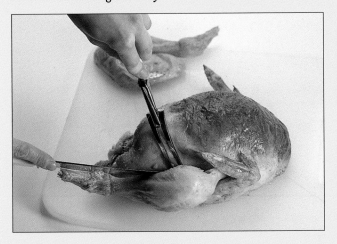

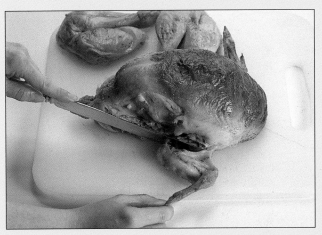

3 *Cut through the joint, keeping the 'oyster' attached. Repeat this procedure with the other leg.*

4 *Use poultry shears or a heavy knife to sever the wing joints.*

5 *Holding the chicken firmly with the fork, carve the breast into slices with a sharp knife, cutting vertically from the top of the chicken parallel with the breast bone.*

Stock making

1 *Place raw or cooked chicken bones and giblets, minus the liver, in a large saucepan and cover with water. Add a bouquet garni, some onion, celery, carrot and a few black peppercorns.*

2 *Bring to the boil, then reduce the heat and simmer for two to three hours. Skim off the scum from the surface.*

3 *Pour the finished stock through a fine sieve and remove the fat before using.*

into thin strips lengthwise, sprinkle with seasoned flour and toss to coat evenly. This is easiest carried out in a plastic bag. Dip each strip into beaten egg, place some breadcrumbs in a plastic bag and add a few egg coated strips at a time, holding the bag closed and shaking it to coat the strips.

Cook goujons for about 3-5 minutes, turning often. Drain well on kitchen paper.

Microwaving
Brush the skin with basting mixtures containing soy sauce, Worcestershire sauce or paprika to make it look brown.

If your microwave manufacturer allows the use of foil, put a strip over the breast or on the leg and wing ends about halfway through cooking to prevent those parts overcooking.

Arrange chicken breasts in one layer in a round microwave dish with the thickest side to the outside of the dish.

Add a little liquid, but no salt as this can make the chicken tough and dry. Cover loosely to speed up cooking and keep the chicken moist. Cook on medium setting to prevent bursting. Turn the chicken over halfway through cooking.

Alternatively, brush breasts or thighs with oil and coat in dry, seasoned breadcrumbs. Place on a microwave rack to cook.

Always allow microwaved chicken to stand a few minutes after cooking.

Chicken can be successfully defrosted by microwave oven. Cover it loosely and turn over during defrosting. Always allow standing time between defrosting and cooking and follow your oven manufacturer's instructions.

Pressure cooking
Calculate cooking time from weight, including stuffing, if used. Pressure cookers cook in about a third of the time of conventional methods.

Chicken bricks
Soak the brick in water for 15 minutes each time before using it. Place in the chicken and start cooking on the lowest oven setting, increasing the heat every 5 minutes until the temperature reaches the required setting in your recipe.

Alternatively, set temperature at 180°C/350°F/Gas Mark 4 and pre-heat the brick for 5 minutes, then put the chicken into it. Raise the oven temperature as the recipe requires and bake the chicken.

Roasting bags
These keep the oven clean and brown chickens very well while keeping them moist. Remember to make a few

slits in the bag to prevent it from exploding. A little flour added to the bag can help with self-basting.

Stuffings for Chicken

(for a 1.6kg/3½lb chicken or 4 poussins)

BASIC BREAD STUFFING

30g/1oz butter or margarine, melted
1 small onion, finely chopped
175g/6oz fresh breadcrumbs
Salt and pepper
2 tsps chopped herbs
1 egg, beaten
Stock or water

Melt butter or margarine and cook the onion to soften. Combine with remaining ingredients, adding enough stock or water to bind the mixture.

Variations:
Cook 2 sticks chopped celery and/or 120g/4oz sliced mushrooms with the onion.
Add 1 apple, cored and chopped, 60g/2oz sultanas and 60g/2oz chopped walnuts.
Cook 225g/8oz sausage meat, and add to the basic stuffing or with any variation or add 6 cooked bacon rashers, diced and cooked or 175g/6oz chopped cooked ham.

CHESTNUT STUFFING

8 bacon rashers, chopped
1 small onion, chopped
30g/1oz butter
120g/4oz fresh breadcrumbs
340-460g/¾-1lb canned unsweetened chestnut purée, softened
1 tbsp chopped parsley
Salt and pepper
1 egg, beaten

Fry bacon and onion in the butter until bacon is crisp. Combine with remaining ingredients, adding just enough egg to bind the mixture.

BASIC RICE STUFFING

30g/1oz butter or margarine
1 small onion, chopped
120g/4oz long-grain rice
280ml/½ pint stock or water
1 tbsp chopped herbs

Melt butter or margarine and cook the onion until softened. Add the rice and cook for 2-3 minutes. Pour on stock or water and bring to the boil. Cover and simmer until the liquid is absorbed and rice is tender.

Variations:
Cook 2 sticks of chopped celery and 120g/4oz sliced mushrooms with the onion and rice. Use ½ the onion and add 175g/6oz seedless, sliced grapes or 120g/4oz chopped, dried apricots and 60g/2oz toasted almonds. Use 60g/2oz wild rice combined with 60g/2oz brown or white rice.

SPICY CRACKED WHEAT STUFFING

120g/4oz bulgar wheat
2 tbsps olive oil
60g/2oz chopped almonds
4 spring onions, chopped
½ tsp ground coriander
½ tsp ground cumin
Pinch of cayenne pepper
60g/2oz raisins
Salt
1 egg, beaten

Pour boiling water over the bulgar wheat to cover. Leave it to soak and absorb most of the water. Heat oil and cook the almonds until pale golden. Add the onions and spices and cook about 1 minute. Combine with the drained bulgar and remaining ingredients, using only enough egg to bind.

Stuffing Boned Chicken

When stuffing a boned chicken (see step-by-step illustrations for method of boning) allow about 675g/1½lbs of stuffing for a 1.6kg/3½lb chicken (whole weight).

Hold the end of the thigh bone and scrape down around the length of it until you get to the place where it joins the drumstick. Cut through the joint to sever the thigh bone but leave the drumstick in place.

Push some of the stuffing well into the spaces left by the removal of the thigh bones and spread the rest over the chicken meat, mounding it in the centre and spreading enough over the neck flap to make it look plump. Make sure you leave enough skin to fold back over. Fold the neck flap and some skin at the tail end, back over the stuffing and bring the sides to the centre to overlap slightly.

Use a trussing needle, threaded with fine twine to sew up the edges with a running stitch. Do not pull the stitches too tight as the stuffing will burst out during cooking. Tie the ends of the twine firmly to secure and turn the chicken over. Plump the chicken up to shape it like a whole chicken, tucking the wing tips under the bird and pushing the drumsticks into the breast.

Truss the bird (see illustrated step-by-step guide) or simply tie the legs together. To carve a cooked bird, simply cut off the wings and legs then slice the body crosswise into thin slices. See **Oven roasting** section for cooking times.

CHAPTER 1

STARTERS
&
PARTY SNACKS

SERVES 4

CHICKEN SATAY

This typical Indonesian dish is very spicy,
and it makes an excellent starter for four.

2 tbsps soy sauce
2 tbsps sesame oil
2 tbsps lime juice
1 tsp ground cumin
1 tsp turmeric powder
2 tsps ground coriander
460g/1lb chicken breast, cut into 2.5cm/1-inch cubes
2 tbsps peanut oil
1 small onion, very finely chopped
1 tsp chilli powder
120g/4oz crunchy peanut butter
1 tsp brown sugar
Lime wedges and coriander leaves, for garnish

1. Put the soy sauce, sesame oil, lime juice, cumin, turmeric and coriander into a large bowl and mix well.

2. Add the cubed chicken to the soy sauce marinade and stir well to coat the meat evenly.

3. Cover and allow to stand in a refrigerator for at least 1 hour, but preferably overnight.

4. Drain the meat, reserving the marinade.

5. Thread the meat onto 4 large or 8 small skewers and set aside.

6. Heat the peanut oil in a small saucepan and add the onion and chilli powder. Cook gently until the onion is slightly softened.

7. Stir the reserved marinade into the oil and onion mixture, along with the peanut butter and brown sugar. Heat gently, stirring constantly, until all the ingredients are well blended. If the sauce is too thick, stir in 2-4 tbsps boiling water.

Step 5 Thread the marinated meat onto 4 large, or 8 small, kebab skewers.

Step 9 Brush the partially grilled chicken with a little of the peanut sauce to baste.

8. Arrange the skewers of meat on a grill pan and cook under a preheated moderate grill for 10-15 minutes. After the first 5 minutes of cooking, brush the skewered meat with a little of the peanut sauce to baste.

9. During the cooking time turn the meat frequently to cook it on all sides and prevent it browning.

10. Serve the skewered meat garnished with the lime and coriander leaves, and hand the remaining sauce separately.

Cook's Notes

Time
Preparation takes about 25 minutes plus at least 1 hour marinating time, cooking takes about 15 minutes.

Serving Idea
Serve with a mixed salad.

SERVES 6-8

TERRINE OF SPINACH AND CHICKEN

This superb terrine is ideal when you want to impress
your guests with a delicious starter.

225g/8oz boned and skinned chicken breasts
2 egg whites
120g/4oz fresh white breadcrumbs
460g/1lb fresh spinach, washed
1 tbsp each of fresh finely chopped chervil, chives
  and tarragon
Salt and pepper
280ml/½ pint double cream
60g/2oz finely chopped walnuts
Pinch nutmeg

Step 2 The spinach should be cooked until it is just wilted, using only the water that clings to the leaves and adding no extra liquid.

1. Cut the chicken into small pieces, then put 1 egg white and half of the breadcrumbs into a food processor and blend until well mixed.

2. Put the spinach into a large saucepan and cover with a tight-fitting lid. Cook for 3 minutes, or until the spinach has just wilted.

3. Remove the chicken mixture from the food processor and rinse the bowl. Put in the spinach along with the herbs, remaining egg white and bread crumbs, and blend until smooth.

4. Season the chicken mixture with salt and pepper and add half of the cream. Mix well to blend thoroughly. Add the remaining cream to the spinach along with the walnuts and the nutmeg. Beat this mixture well to blend thoroughly.

5. Line a 460g/1lb loaf tin with greaseproof paper. Lightly oil this with a little vegetable oil. Pour the chicken mixture into the base of the tin and spread evenly.

6. Carefully pour the spinach mixture over the chicken mixture, and smooth the top with a palette knife. Cover the tin with lightly oiled foil and seal this tightly around the edges.

7. Stand the tin in a roasting dish and pour enough warm water into the dish to come halfway up the sides of the tin. Cook in a preheated 160°C/325°F/Gas Mark 3 oven for 1 hour, or until it is firm.

8. Cool the terrine, then refrigerate for at least 12 hours. Carefully lift the terrine out of the tin and peel off the paper. To serve, cut the terrine into thin slices with a sharp knife.

Cook's Notes

Time
Preparation takes 25 minutes, cooking takes 1 hour.

 Serving Idea
Serve slices of the terrine on individual serving plates garnished with a little salad.

! **Watchpoint**
Do not overcook the terrine or attempt to cook it any more quickly than the recipe states, otherwise it will curdle and spoil.

SERVES 6

CHICKEN STUFFED PEPPERS

Try a stuffing that is different from the
usual meat and rice one for light tasting peppers.

3 large green or red peppers
60g/2oz butter or margarine
1 small onion, finely chopped
1 stick celery, finely chopped
1 clove garlic, crushed
3 chicken breasts, skinned, boned and diced
2 tsps chopped parsley
Salt and pepper
½ loaf of stale bread, made into crumbs
1-2 eggs, beaten
60g/6 tbsps dry breadcrumbs

Step 1 Cut peppers in half and remove seeds and white core.

1. Cut the pepper in half lengthwise and remove the cores and seeds. Leave the stems attached, if wished.

2. Melt the butter in a frying pan and add the onion, celery, garlic and chicken. Cook over moderate heat until the vegetables are softened and the chicken is cooked. Add the parsley. Season with salt and pepper.

3. Stir in the stale breadcrumbs and add enough beaten egg to make the mixture hold together.

Step 4 Spoon filling into the pepper halves, mounding the top and smoothing out.

4. Spoon filling into each pepper half, mounding the top slightly. Place the peppers in a baking dish that holds them closely.

5. Pour enough water down the inside of the dish to come about 1.25cm/½ inch up the sides of the peppers. Cover and bake in an oven pre-heated to 180°C/350°F/Gas Mark 4 for about 45 minutes, or until the peppers are just tender.

6. Sprinkle each with the dried breadcrumbs and place under a preheated grill until golden brown.

Step 5 Place peppers close together in a baking dish and carefully pour in about 1.25cm/½ inch water.

Cook's Notes

 Time
Preparation takes about 30 minutes and cooking takes about 45-50 minutes.

 Variations
Use spring onions in place of the small onion. Add chopped nuts or black olives to the filling, if wished.

 Serving Idea
Serve as a first course, either hot or cold, or as a light lunch or supper with a salad.

SERVES 4

CHICKEN LIVER PÂTÉ

Deceptively quick and easy to prepare, this
creamy pâté is sure to be a firm favourite.

30g/1oz butter, for frying
1 clove garlic, crushed
1 onion, finely chopped
Salt and pepper
225g/8oz chicken livers, trimmed
1 tsp Worcestershire sauce
60g/2oz butter, creamed
1 tbsp brandy

Step 5 Add the
creamed butter
and brandy to the
processed chicken
livers and blend
until completely
smooth.

Step 2 Increase
the heat and sauté
the chicken livers
in the hot butter
and onions for
about 2 minutes,
stirring until they
are just cooked
through.

2. Increase the heat and stir in the chicken livers. Sauté
for about 2 minutes on each side, stirring continuously,
until just cooked through.

3. Add the Worcestershire sauce and stir.

4. Put the contents of the frying pan into a food
process, or liquidizer, and blend for ½-1 minute until just
smooth.

5. Add the creamed butter and the brandy to the
processor and process again until the pâté is smooth.

6. Transfer the pâté to 1 large dish, or 4 individual
serving dishes, and refrigerate until required.

1. Heat the butter in a frying pan and add the garlic,
onion, salt and pepper. Sauté gently, until the onions
have softened, but not coloured.

Cook's Notes

 Time
Preparation takes about 15
minutes and cooking takes
15 minutes.

Preparation
If you do not have a liquidizer
or food processor, the
cooked chicken livers can be
pressed through a wire sieve, using
the back of a spoon, into a bowl; then
beat in the butter and brandy to
achieve the creamed pâté mixture.

Cook's Tip
This pâté can be prepared in
advance, but if you are not
eating it straight away, seal the
surface with clarified butter and
refrigerate until required.

SERVES 4

ORANGE AND CARDAMOM CHICKEN WINGS

The rather mysterious, perfumed flavour of cardamom is intriguing enough to use without many other ingredients, and almost everyone likes it.

8 chicken wings
4 cloves garlic, crushed
Finely grated rind 1 large orange
90ml/6 tbsps orange juice
1 tbsp lemon juice
60ml/4 tbsps oil
Seeds from 10 cardamom pods, crushed
Salt and freshly ground black pepper

1. Wipe the chicken wings with some kitchen paper and cut off and discard the tips. Put the wings into a shallow ovenproof dish.

2. Mix the remaining ingredients together, pour over the chicken and allow to marinate for at least 4 hours covered or up to 24 hours in the refrigerator.

3. Allow the chicken to come to room temperature, then cook uncovered at 200°C/400°F/Gas Mark 6, for about 30 minutes, basting one or twice. Serve hot or cold.

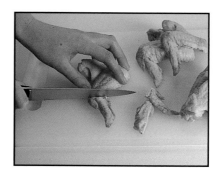

Step 1 Cut the tips off the chicken wings with a sharp knife.

Step 2 Mix all the ingredients together and pour over the chicken, to marinate for at least 4 hours.

Cook's Notes

Time
Preparation takes about 25 minutes, plus a minimum of 4 hours marinating time. Cooking takes about 30 minutes.

Serving Idea
Serve as a party snack or a picnic treat.

Cook's Tip
The chicken wings should be allowed to come to room temperature before cooking else they will take longer to cook.

SERVES 8

SESAME CHICKEN WINGS

This is an economical starter that is also good as a
cocktail snack or as a light meal with stir-fried vegetables.

12 chicken wings
1 tbsp salted black beans
1 tbsp boiling water
1 tbsp oil
2 cloves garlic, crushed
2 slices fresh root ginger, cut into fine shreds
3 tbsps soy sauce
1½ tbsps rice wine or dry sherry
Large pinch black pepper
1 tbsp sesame seeds

1. Cut off and discard the wing tips. Cut between the join to separate into two pieces.

2. Crush the beans and add the water. Leave to stand.

3. Heat the oil in a wok and add the garlic and ginger. Stir briefly and add the chicken wings. Cook, stirring, until lightly browned, for about 3 minutes. Add the soy sauce and wine and cook, stirring, for about 30 seconds longer. Add the soaked black beans and pepper.

4. Cover the wok tightly and allow to simmer for about 8-10 minutes. Uncover and turn the heat to high. Continue cooking, stirring until the liquid is almost evaporated and the chicken wings are glazed with sauce. Remove

Step 1 Use a knife or scissors to cut through thick joint and separate the wing into two pieces.

Step 3 Fry garlic and ginger briefly, add the chicken wings and cook, stirring, until lightly browned.

from the heat and sprinkle on sesame seeds. Stir to coat completely and serve. Garnish with spring onions or coriander, if wished.

Cook's Notes

Time
Preparation takes about 25 minutes, cooking takes about 13-14 minutes.

Cook's Tip
You can prepare the chicken wings ahead of time and reheat them. They are best reheated in the oven for about 10 minutes at 180°C/350°F/Gas Mark 4.

Serving Idea
To garnish with spring onion brushes, trim the roots and green tops of spring onions and cut both ends into thin strips, leaving the middle intact. Place in ice water for several hours or overnight for the cut ends to curl up. Drain and use to garnish.

SERVES 4

PLUM-GLAZED CHICKEN WINGS

This dish is extremely versatile. It can be cooked under the grill,
in the oven or on the barbecue, and is delicious hot or cold.

8 chicken wings
½ onion, sliced
2-3 cloves garlic, chopped
1 bay leaf
2 star anise

Glaze
3 heaped tbsps plum jam
1 tsp five spice powder
1 tbsp vinegar, cider or wine

Step 2 Mix together the plum jam, five spice powder and vinegar.

Step 1 Simmer the chicken wings in water with the onion, garlic, bay leaf, and star anise.

Step 3 Arrange the wings on a grill pan and paint with half the plum jam mixture.

1. Put the chicken wings in a saucepan together with the onion, garlic, bay leaf and star anise. Cover with cold water, bring to the boil and simmer for 10 minutes.

2. Mix together the jam, five spice powder and vinegar, cider or wine.

3. Put the drained wings on to the rack of a grill pan and paint with half the jam mixture. Grill under a high heat for 10 minutes, basting several times.

4. Turn the wings, brush with the remaining jam and continue cooking for a further 10 minutes until very brown, taking care not to burn the jam. Alternatively, the wings may be cooked in the oven at 220°C/425°F/Gas Mark 7 for 15 minutes, then for a further 15 minutes after the second coating of jam. Serve the wings hot or cold.

Cook's Notes

Time
Preparation takes about 10 minutes, cooking takes about 30 minutes.

Serving Idea
For a barbecue, a great accompaniment would be hot jacket potatoes with butter. Alternatively, serve on a bed of plain boiled rice.

Cook's Tip
If cooking these on a barbecue, be careful not to serve them immediately as the jam gets very hot and will easily burn unwary mouths.

CHAPTER 2

LIGHT MEALS & SALADS

SERVES 4-8

CHINESE LEAF CHICKEN STIR-FRY SALAD

A more substantial version of the warm salads
which many restaurants serve as a first course.

60ml/4 tbsps olive oil
3 cloves garlic, crushed
460g/1lb chicken breast, skinned and cut into 1cm/
    ½-inch wide strips
225g/8oz Chinese leaves, shredded
½ cucumber, cut into 5cm/2-inch sticks
1 green pepper, cut into thin 5cm/2-inch strips
2 sticks celery, cut into thin 5cm/2-inch strips
1 tbsp parsley
2-3 tbsps dry vermouth
Salt and freshly ground black pepper

1. Heat 3 tablespoons of the oil in a wok or frying pan
and stir-fry the garlic and chicken over a medium high
heat for 10 minutes or until tender and lightly browned but
cooked through. Remove the chicken and keep warm.

2. Add the Chinese leaves, cucumber, pepper and

celery to the pan with the remaining oil and stir-fry for
2-3 minutes.

3. Turn the mixture onto a heated serving dish or
individual plates, then arrange the chicken on top.

4. Add the parsley and vermouth to the pan and scrape
any browned pan juices from the bottom. Season, pour
over the chicken and vegetables and serve at once.

Step 2 Add the
Chinese leaves,
cucumber, pepper
and celery, with the
remaining oil and
stir-fry for 2-3
minutes.

Step 1 Stir-fry the
garlic and chicken
strips over a
medium heat for
about 10 minutes
or until lightly
browned and
cooked.

Step 4 Add the
parsley and
vermouth to the
pan and scrape up
any browned pan
juices.

Cook's Notes

 Time
Preparation takes about 5
minutes, and cooking takes
about 15 minutes.

 Variation
Courgettes can be
substituted for the cucumber.

 Serving Idea
Serve as a warm salad
amongst 6 or 8, or as an
attractive dinner or lunch for 4. It is
essential to serve this dish
immediately or the fresh crunch of the
green vegetables, in contrast with the
succulent chicken, will be lost.

SERVES 4

CORONATION CHICKEN

This delicious, creamy dish is perfect fare
for that special summer picnic.

275g/10oz fromage frais or Quark
3-4 tbsps mayonnaise
½-1 tsp curry paste (according to taste)
2 tbsps apricot & ginger or mango chutney
460g/1lb cooked chicken, diced
1 medium can apricot halves in natural juice, drained
30g/1oz flaked almonds, toasted
Parsley for garnish

Step 2 Add diced
cooked chicken to
the dressing.

Step 1 Mix
fromage frais,
mayonnaise, curry
paste and chutney
together well.

Step 3 Chop half
the apricots and
add to the chicken.

1. Mix together the fromage frais, mayonnaise, curry paste and chutney in a large bowl until the curry is well blended. Taste and add more curry paste if required.

2. Add diced chicken meat.

3. Chop half of the apricots and add to the mixture.

4. Pile onto a serving plate and chill before serving. Garnish with the remaining apricots, sliced, and sprinkle with toasted almonds. Add some parsley sprigs if wished.

Cook's Notes

Time
Preparation takes 10-15
minutes plus chilling time.

Variation
Use canned mango or
pineapple, instead of
apricots.

Watchpoint
Do not add the toasted
almonds until serving time else
they will become soggy.

SERVES 4

TARRAGON CHICKEN PANCAKES

These attractive pancakes look sophisticated enough
for a dinner party, but are also so easy to make,
you can indulge yourself at any time.

120g/4oz plain wholemeal flour
1 egg
280ml/½ pint milk
Oil, for frying
45g/1½oz plain flour
280ml/½ pint milk
Salt and black pepper, to taste
225g/8oz cooked chicken, chopped
1 avocado pear, peeled, halved, stoned and chopped
2 tsps lemon juice
1 tbsp chopped fresh tarragon

1. Put the wholemeal flour into a large bowl, and make a slight well in the centre. Break the egg into the well and begin to beat the egg carefully into the flour, incorporating only a little flour at a time.

2. Add the milk gradually to the egg and flour mixture, beating well between additions, until all the milk is incorporated and the batter is smooth.

3. Heat a little oil in a small frying pan, or crêpe pan, and cook about 2 tbsps of the batter at a time, tipping and rotating the pan, so that the batter spreads evenly over the base to form a pancake. Flip the pancake over, to cook the second side.

4. Repeat this process until all the batter has been used up. Keep the pancakes warm, until required.

5. Blend the plain flour with a little of the milk, and gradually add the rest of the milk, until it is all incorporated.

6. Pour the flour and milk mixture into a small pan, and cook over a moderate heat, stirring continuously, until the sauce has thickened. Season to taste.

7. Stir the chopped chicken, avocado, lemon juice and tarragon into the sauce.

8. Fold each pancake in half, and then in half again, to form a triangle.

9. Carefully open part of the triangle out to form an envelope, and fill this with the chicken and avocado mixture.

Step 1 Put the flour into a bowl and make a slight well in the centre. Break the egg into this well, and beat gently, incorporating a little of the flour at a time.

Step 3 Using a small frying pan, or crêpe pan, heat a little hot oil and fry 2 tbsps of the batter at a time. Tip and rotate the pan whilst cooking, to distribute the batter evenly over the base, and make a nice thin pancake.

Cook's Notes

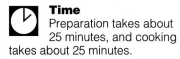

Time
Preparation takes about 25 minutes, and cooking takes about 25 minutes.

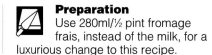

Preparation
Use 280ml/½ pint fromage frais, instead of the milk, for a luxurious change to this recipe.

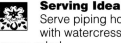

Serving Idea
Serve piping hot, garnished with watercress and a crisp green salad.

SERVES 4

CHICKEN SALAD WITH MANGO AND SOURED CREAM DRESSING

This recipe is a perfect way of turning leftover chicken into a delicious main course dish.

2 tbsps fresh chives, chopped, or 1 tbsp dried chives
60ml/4 tbsps dry white wine
100ml/4 heaped tbsps good mayonnaise
100ml/4 heaped tbsps soured cream
Scant 1 tsp powdered mustard
Salt and freshly ground black pepper
1-2 mangoes, depending on size
460g/1lb cooked chicken breast, skinned and boned

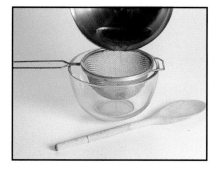

Step 2 Sieve the chive mixture, pressing the chives to extract as much of their essence as possible.

Step 1 Simmer the chives and wine for 5 minutes or until reduced to 1-2 tablespoons.

Step 5 Slice the chicken into roughly the same size pieces as the mango.

1. Put the chives, with the wine, into a small pan and simmer, uncovered, for about 5 minutes, until reduced to only 1 or 2 tablespoons.

2. Pour through a fine sieve, pushing the chives to extract as much of their essence as possible.

3. Mix the mayonnaise with the soured cream, mustard and about 1 tablespoon of the chive essence. Don't let the dressing become too thin, particularly if the dish is being made in advance.

4. Check the seasoning, adding salt and pepper if necessary.

5. Peel and slice the mango and cut the cold chicken into slices of approximately the same size.

6. Arrange roughly in a shallow dish and pour the dressing over, tossing lightly so that all the pieces are covered.

Cook's Notes

Time
Preparation takes about 25 minutes.

Serving Idea
This salad is delicious when served with a chilled Chardonnay wine.

Cook's Tip
If making this salad in advance do not coat with the dressing until serving time.

SERVES 4

CURRIED CHICKEN DRUMSTICKS

This Tandoori recipe appeals to all age groups and is perfect for barbecues or for informal parties as it can be made in large quantities.

8 chicken drumsticks
Juice of 2 lemons
4 large cloves garlic, crushed
2.5cm/1-inch piece of root ginger, peeled and finely chopped
1 generous tsp ground cumin
2 tsps sweet paprika
2 tsps ground coriander
140ml/¼ pint natural yogurt
¼ tsp chilli powder or cayenne pepper

Step 2 Put the chicken into a shallow dish and sprinkle with half the lemon juice.

Step 1 Dry the drumsticks, then score with a sharp knife.

1. Wipe the drumsticks with some kitchen paper and score with a sharp knife in several places.

2. Sprinkle with half the lemon juice and put into a shallow dish. Mix the remaining ingredients together and spread evenly over the chicken. Cover the dish and leave to marinate overnight in the refrigerator.

3. Transfer the chicken to a foil-lined baking tin and cook, uncovered in an oven preheated to 200°C/400°F/Gas Mark 6, for 30 minutes, turning halfway through.

4. Baste the chicken and put under a hot grill or on a barbecue for 10-15 minutes, turning and basting frequently until very brown.

Step 4 Transfer the chicken to a grill pan and baste with some of the marinade.

Cook's Notes

Time
Preparation takes about 15 minutes, plus overnight marinating time. Cooking takes about 40-45 minutes.

Variation
If liked, red food colouring may be added to the marinade for an authentic appearance, although this will not affect the flavour. For extra heat add more chilli powder, or some mustard oil.

Serving Idea
Serve the chicken with lemon and cucumber and a dressing of natural yogurt into which you have stirred lots of chopped fresh mint.

SERVES 4

CHICKEN AND AVOCADO SALAD

The creamy herb dressing complements this easy summer salad.

8 anchovy fillets, soaked in milk, rinsed and dried
1 spring onion, chopped
2 tbsps chopped fresh tarragon
3 tbsps chopped chives
15g/4 tbsps chopped parsley
280ml/½ pint prepared mayonnaise
140ml/¼ pint natural yogurt
2 tbsps tarragon vinegar
Pinch sugar and cayenne pepper
1 large head lettuce
460g/1lb cooked chicken
1 avocado, peeled and sliced or cubed
1 tbsp lemon juice

1. Combine all the ingredients, except the lettuce, chicken, avocado and lemon juice in a food processor. Work the ingredients until smooth, and well mixed. Leave in the refrigerator at least 1 hour for the flavours to blend.

2. Shred the lettuce or tear into bite-size pieces and arrange on plates.

3. Top the lettuce with the cooked chicken, cut into strips or cubes.

4. Spoon the dressing over the chicken. Brush the avocado slices, or toss the cubes, with lemon juice and garnish the salad. Serve any remaining dressing separately.

Step 1 The dressing should be very well blended after working in a food processor. Alternatively, use a hand blender.

Step 3 Arrange lettuce on individual plates and top with shredded chicken.

Cook's Notes

Time
Preparation takes about 30 minutes, plus 1 hour standing time.

Preparation
Dressing may be prepared ahead of time and kept in the refrigerator for a day or two.

Serving Idea
The dressing may be served as a dip for vegetable crudités or with a tossed salad.

SERVES 4

APRICOT CHICKEN WITH MINT

This is a delicious recipe with a light, yogurt-based sauce of
the most beguilling pale apricot colour and fascinating
clear flavour. It can be served hot or cold.

8 chicken thighs or drumsticks, skinned
60g/2oz onion, finely chopped
1 orange
2 tbsps lemon juice
60g/2oz dried apricots
2 tbsps chopped fresh mint or 2 tsps dried mint
140ml/¼ pint dry white wine
Salt and freshly ground black pepper
3-4 tbsps thick natural yogurt, to serve

1. Put the chicken into a flameproof casserole and add
the onion, finely grated rind of the orange with 60ml/4
tbsps of juice, and the remaining ingredients except the
yogurt. Be generous with the mint, as much of the flavour
cooks away.

Step 1 Cover the
chicken with the
onion, orange rind
and juice and add
the remaining
ingredients. Add
plenty of mint.

2. Cover and marinate for 2-4 hours or overnight, in the
refrigerator.

3. Allow the chicken to come to room temperature, then
bake covered, in a preheated oven to 190°C/375°F/Gas
Mark 5, for 45 minutes or until tender. Remove the
chicken and keep warm.

Step 4 Sieve the
puréed sauce,
using the back of a
soup ladle for
speed, into a
saucepan.

4. Purée the rest of the casserole contents in a food
processor or liquidiser and then force through a sieve
(using the back of a soup ladle for efficiency and speed)
into a saucepan.

5. Reheat but do not boil. Remove from the heat and
stir in the yogurt, tasting all the time to get a pouring
sauce that is rich but light in flavour. Adjust the seasoning
with salt and pepper then pour the sauce over the
chicken.

Cook's Notes

Time
Preparation takes about 25
minute, plus minimum of 2
hours marinating time. Cooking
takes about 45 minutes.

Variation
You can serve this dish cold
for a buffet, in which case
you should cool the chicken and the
sauce separately.

Serving Idea
You can serve the dish hot,
with the sauce in a separate
container as a dip. In both cases, it is
ideal with a mixed green salad.

SERVES 4

SAFFRON CHICKEN QUICHE

The exciting contrast of rich chicken and warm spices with the
sharpness of lemon and parsley is bridged by a sprinkle of sugar.

22.5-25 x 5cm/9-10 x 2 inch flan dish, lined with rich
   shortcrust pastry
8 eggs
60g/2oz butter
60g/2oz onion, finely chopped
90ml/6 tbsps lemon juice
3 sachets powdered saffron
340g/12oz uncooked chicken meat, cut into long,
   strips
2 tsps ground cinnamon
½ tsp white pepper
15g/½oz fresh parsley, including stalks, coarsely
   chopped
1 tsp sugar

Step 2 Paint the hot pastry case with the egg white to seal it.

Step 3 Melt the butter, add the onion, lemon juice and saffron, and cook gently until the onion is soft.

1. Line the pastry case with greaseproof paper and cover with baking beans (or use dried kidney beans, pasta or rice), to bake blind. Put into a preheated oven, 200°C/400°F/Gas Mark 6 and bake for 10 minutes. Remove the beans, carefully take off the greaseproof paper and return to the oven for a further 10 minutes until the base is set.

2. Lightly whisk a white from one of the eggs and paint this on to the hot pastry; return to the oven for a few minutes to ensure it sets and seals the pastry.

3. Melt the butter, add the onion, lemon juice and saffron and cook gently until the onion is really soft.

4. Stir in the chicken meat, cook gently for 5 minutes then set aside to cool.

5. Beat the cinnamon and white pepper into the eggs and

stir in the parsley and the juices from the cooked chicken.

6. Arrange the chicken neatly on the cooled pastry case and ladle on the egg mixture. Transfer to a preheated oven, 160°C/325°F/Gas Mark 3, for 15 minutes.

7. Sprinkle with sugar and return to the oven for a further 25 minutes, until lightly browned just around the edges and only just set – it will firm up more once out of the oven. (If you overcook the flan, the eggs will toughen.) Serve warm or cold.

Cook's Notes

 Time
Preparation, including blind baking the pastry, takes about 25 minutes, cooking takes about 40 minutes.

Serving Idea
Serve warm or lightly chilled at buffets or picnics, as either a first or main course.

 Variation
If you cannot find saffron but like the yellow colour, you can substitute turmeric, but it will not give quite the same flavour.

SERVES 4-6

LEFTOVER CHICKEN SALAD

This recipe is perfect for using up leftovers of cooked chicken.

2 ripe but firm avocados, or 1 mango
Lemon juice
4 tomatoes, skinned
460g/1lb cooked chicken meat, broken or cut into
 small cubes
2 spring onions, chopped
2 tbsps chopped parsley
60g/2oz roasted cashew nuts
Parsley to garnish

For the Garlic Vinaigrette
3 tbsps groundnut oil
1 tbsp white wine vinegar
1 tsp Fresh mustard
1 clove garlic, crushed
½ tsp caster sugar
Salt and freshly ground black pepper

1. Split the avocado in half, remove the stone and skin and cut the flesh into neat slices. Brush with lemon juice to prevent discolouration. If using mango instead, peel and cut the flesh into neat slices.

2. Slice the tomatoes and arrange alternately with the avocado or mango around the outer edge of a flat serving dish.

3. Mix the chicken with the spring onions, parsley and nuts.

4. Whisk together the garlic vinaigrette ingredients and use enough to coat the chicken well. Pile the mixture in the centre of the avocado or mango and tomato.

5. Brush the avocado or mango and tomato with a little dressing and sprinkle everything lightly with chopped parsley.

Step 1 Brush the sliced avocado with lemon juice to prevent discolouration.

Step 3 Mix together the cooked chicken, spring onions, parsley and nuts.

Step 4 Pour enough vinaigrette over the chicken to coat it well.

Cook's Notes

Time
Preparation takes about 25 minutes.

Variation
Use paw paws, kiwi fruit or peaches in place of the avocado.

Serving Idea
Serve the salad with granary bread and butter and a chilled dry white wine.

SERVES 4

HERBY LEMON CHICKEN

Served either hot or cold, this refreshing recipe
is perfect for picnics and light suppers.

175g/6oz fresh white breadcrumbs
2 tbsps chopped parsley
2 tbsps chopped tarragon
Zest 1 lemon
Salt and freshly ground black pepper
1 tbsp Dijon mustard
60g/2oz butter
8 chicken drumsticks, skinned
Flour for dusting
1 egg, size 2, beaten

For the lemon and herb butter
120g/4oz butter, slightly salted
Zest ½ lemon
Squeeze lemon juice
2 tbsps chopped parsley
2 tbsps chopped tarragon

Step 1 Mix breadcrumbs, parsley, tarragon and lemon zest together.

1. Put the breadcrumbs in a large, shallow bowl and add the parsley, tarragon and lemon zest. Season with salt and pepper and mix well.

2. Put the mustard and butter together in a saucepan and melt. Remove from the heat and add the breadcrumb mixture, stirring well to coat all the breadcrumbs in butter. Cool.

3. Coat each drumstick, one at a time, with flour. Dip, one at a time, in the beaten egg and then roll in the breadcrumbs, pressing the mixture on gently to give an even coating.

4. Lay the drumsticks on a rack over a roasting tin and bake in an oven preheated to 200°C/400°F/Gas Mark 6 for 30-40 minutes, or until golden and crisp.

5. Meanwhile, thoroughly mix together all the lemon and herb butter ingredients. Place on a piece of greaseproof paper and pat into a cylinder using a knife. Roll up the butter inside the paper and twist the ends to seal. Chill until firm. To serve, unwrap and slice into rounds to accompany the chicken.

Step 3 Dust each drumstick with flour.

Step 3 Coat with breadcrumb mixture, pressing on gently to give an even coating.

Cook's Notes

Time
Preparation takes about 25 minutes, cooking takes about 30-40 minutes.

Variation
You could substitute fresh brown breadcrumbs for white and experiment by using your own favourite herbs.

Serving Idea
Serve hot with herb butter and a slice of lemon, or cold with a green salad.

SERVES 4

CHICKEN LIVERS WITH CHINESE LEAVES & ALMONDS

Chicken livers need quick cooking so are perfect for stir-frying.

225g/8oz chicken livers
3 tbsps oil
60g/2oz split blanched almonds
1 clove garlic, peeled
60g/2oz mange tout peas
8-10 Chinese leaves, finely shredded
2 tsps cornflour mixed with 1 tbsp cold water
2 tbsps soy sauce
140ml/¼ pint chicken stock

Step 2 Cook the almonds slowly in the oil to brown evenly, stirring often.

Step 1 Cut off any yellowish or greenish portions from the livers and divide them into even-sized pieces.

Step 3 Quickly stir-fry the livers until lightly brown on the outside. May be served slightly pink in the middle.

1. Pick over the chicken livers and remove any discoloured areas or bits of fat. Cut the chicken livers into even-sized pieces.

2. Heat a wok and pour in the oil. When the oil is hot, turn the heat down and add the almonds. Cook, stirring continuously, over gentle heat until the almonds are a nice golden brown. Remove and drain on kitchen paper.

3. Add the garlic, cook for 1-2 minutes to flavour the oil and remove. Add the chicken livers and cook for

about 2-3 minutes, stirring frequently. Remove the chicken livers and set them aside. Add the mange tout to the wok and stir-fry for 1 minute. Add the Chinese leaves to the wok and cook for 1 minute. Remove the vegetables and set them aside.

4. Mix together the cornflour and water with the soy sauce and stock. Pour into the wok and bring to the boil. Cook until thickened and clear. Return all the other ingredients to the sauce and reheat for 30 seconds. Serve immediately.

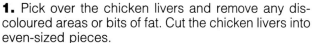

Cook's Notes

 Time
Preparation takes about 25 minutes, cooking takes about 10 minutes.

 Preparation
Remove any discoloured portions from the livers as these can cause a bitter taste. Livers may be served slightly pink in the middle.

 Serving Idea
Serve with plain or fried rice. Chinese noodles also make a good accompaniment.

SERVES 6

MEXICAN CHICKEN & PEPPER SALAD

This is the perfect lunch or light supper dish during the summer.

460g/1lb cooked chicken, cut in strips
140ml/¼ pint mayonnaise
140ml/¼ pint natural yogurt
1 tsp chilli powder
1 tsp paprika
Pinch cayenne pepper
½ tsp tomato purée
1 tsp onion purée
1 green pepper, finely sliced
1 red pepper, finely sliced
175g/6oz frozen sweetcorn, defrosted
175g/6oz long grain rice, cooked, to serve

1. Place the chicken strips in a large salad bowl.

2. Mix the mayonnaise, yogurt, spices, tomato and onion purées together and leave to stand briefly for flavours to blend. Fold dressing into the chicken.

3. Add the pepper and sweetcorn and mix gently until all the ingredients are coated with dressing.

4. Place the rice on a serving dish and pile the salad into the centre. Serve immediately.

Step 3 Fold all ingredients together gently so that they do not break up. Use a large spoon or rubber spatula.

Step 4 Arrange rice on a serving plate and spoon salad into the centre.

Cook's Notes

Time
Preparation takes about 30 minutes.

Buying Guide
Onion purée is available in tubes like tomato purée.

Preparation
Chicken salad may be prepared several hours in advance and kept covered in the refrigerator. Spoon onto rice just before serving.

Variation
Add sliced green chillies or Jalapeno peppers for hotter flavour. Try chilli sauce or taco sauce as an alternative seasoning.

SERVES 4

MANGO CHICKEN THIGHS OR DRUMSTICKS WITH COCONUT

Slightly piquant and immensely satisfying and simple to make. Ideal cold in picnic hampers.

8 chicken thighs or drumsticks
175ml/6oz mango chutney
30g/1oz desiccated coconut
1 tsp mild curry paste
Lemon juice

1. Skin the chicken pieces and with a sharp knife make a 2.5cm/1-inch slit along the bone.

2. Cut the flesh each side of the bone to make two small pockets, but don't cut all the way through.

3. Put the mango chutney into a sieve standing over a bowl and separate the solids from the sauce.

4. Chop the mango flesh roughly, mix with the coconut and curry paste and add a squeeze of lemon juice.

5. Stuff the pockets with the mixture and place them in a lightly oiled or greased baking dish.

Step 1 Skin the chicken thighs or drumsticks with a sharp knife.

Step 5 Stuff the pockets with the mango mixture.

Step 6 Brush half the sauce over the chicken thighs before cooking.

6. Stir a squeeze of lemon juice into the reserved sauce from the mango chutney and brush half of this over the thighs.

7. Bake uncovered in an oven preheated to 200°C/400°F/Gas Mark 6 for 15 minutes, then brush with the remaining sauce and return to the oven for a further 15 minutes, or until cooked through and tender.

Cook's Notes

Time
Preparation takes about 15 minutes and cooking takes about 30 minutes.

Variation
This recipe can be varied by using peach chutney or any other chutney that has large, solid pieces of fruit in it.

Serving Idea
Choose the thighs if you are eating at a table, perhaps with a salad as either a first or main course. The drumsticks are ideal for picnics and buffets.

SERVES 4

SUMMER PICNIC PARMESAN AND HERB CHICKEN

This dish is fabulous served cold, when the flavours have had time
to mingle and develop. It is also good served warm – especially
in summer – with a chilled dry rosé wine from Provence.

60g/2oz Parmesan cheese, grated
30g/1oz ground almonds
60ml/4 tbsps olive oil
30g/1oz fresh garlic, or rather less if old
15g/½oz fresh basil
1 x 1.4kg/3lb chicken
1 tbsp extra Parmesan

4. Rub the extra Parmesan into the skin before putting
the bird into a roasting bag, or a roasting dish which you
can cover with a lid or foil.

5. Bake at 190°C/375°F/Gas mark 5 for 20 minutes per
460g/1lb, plus 20 minutes extra.

Step 3 Press the
stuffing under the
skin, as evenly as
possible, to cover
the breast meat
and part of the
legs.

Step 2 Gently
ease the chicken
skin away from the
flesh, starting
around the
wishbone.

Step 4 Rub the
extra parmesan,
into the skin before
cooking.

1. Mix together the cheese, almonds and oil to form a
soft paste. Finely slice the garlic and chop the basil very
roughly. Stir these into the paste.

2. Gently ease the chicken skin away from the flesh,
starting around the wishbone.

3. Press the stuffing under the skin as evenly as you can,
covering the whole of the breast and some of the legs.
Pat the skin back over the bird.

Cook's Notes

 Time
Preparation takes about 25
minutes and cooking takes
about 1 hour 20 minutes.

 Serving Idea
Serve with a lovely, crisp,
green salad.

 Variation
Substitute any fresh herb like
mint or parsley for the basil –
the dish will be equally delicious.

CHAPTER 3

FAMILY MAIN MEALS

SERVES 6

HONEY AND LEMON CHICKEN

Roast chicken is a firm favourite with everyone and this
simple recipe is a delicious alternative to the traditional roast.

1 onion, finely chopped
25g/6 tbsps wholemeal breadcrumbs
Grated rind and juice of 1 lemon
1 egg, beaten
Salt and pepper
1 x 1.6kg/3½lb chicken
2 tbsps clear honey
Parsley and lemon slices for garnish

Step 2 Stuff chicken at the neck end.

Step 1 Combine onion, bread-crumbs, half the lemon rind and juice, and egg for the stuffing.

Step 3 Brush well with honey and lemon juice 30 minutes before the end of cooking time.

1. Make a stuffing mixture by combining the finely chopped onion, breadcrumbs, half of the lemon rind and juice and the beaten egg, adding salt and pepper to taste.

2. Stuff the chicken at the neck end then brush with a little melted butter or margarine, cover with foil and cook for 20 minutes per 460g/1lb 180°C/350°F/Gas Mark 4, plus 20 minutes extra.

3. Thirty minutes before the end of cooking, take the chicken out of the oven, remove the foil and brush liberally with a mixture of the clear honey and remaining lemon juice. Return to the oven until chicken is cooked and golden. Serve garnished with parsley and lemon slices.

Cook's Notes

Time
Preparation takes about 15 minutes, cooking will take about 1 hour 40 minutes.

Serving Idea
Serve as a traditional roast or enjoy cold, when the lemon flavour really comes through.

Cook's Tip
When calculating the cooking time, remember to use the stuffed weight of the chicken.

SERVES 4-6

CHICKEN AND SAUSAGE RISOTTO

This is really a one pot meal and one
you won't have to cook in the oven.

1.4kg/3lbs chicken portions, skinned, boned, and cut
  into cubes
1ltr/1¾ pints water
45g/1½oz butter or margarine
1 large onion, roughly chopped
3 sticks celery, roughly chopped
1 large green pepper, roughly chopped
1 clove garlic, crushed
Salt and pepper
225g/8oz uncooked rice
400g/14oz can tomatoes
175g/6oz smoked sausage, cut into 1.25cm/½ inch dice
Chopped parsley

1. Use the chicken skin and bones, onion and celery trimmings to make stock. Cover ingredients with the water, bring to the boil and simmer slowly for 1 hour. Strain and reserve.

2. Melt the butter or margarine in a large saucepan and add the onion. Cook slowly to brown and then add the celery, green pepper and garlic and cook briefly.

3. Add salt and pepper and the rice, stirring to mix well.

4. Add the chicken, tomatoes, sausage and 850ml/1½ pints of the stock and mix well. Bring to the boil, reduce the heat to simmering and cook about 20-25 minutes, stirring occasionally until the chicken is done and the rice is tender. The rice should have absorbed most of the liquid by the time it has cooked. Garnish with chopped parsley.

Remove the skin from the chicken and set aside.

Step 1 Put the skin and bones in a large stock pot with the onion and celery trimmings to make the stock. Add water to cover.

Cook's Notes

Time
Preparation takes about 35-40 minutes and cooking takes about 20-25 minutes.

Preparation
Check the level of liquid occasionally as the rice is cooking and add more water or stock as necessary. If there is a lot of liquid left and the rice is nearly cooked, uncover the pan and boil rapidly.

Serving Idea
Accompany with a green salad to make a complete meal.

SERVES 6

CHICKEN COBBLER

This dish is warming winter fare with its
creamy sauce and tender, light topping.

4 chicken joints, 2 breasts and 2 legs
1.5 litres/2½ pints water
1 bay leaf
4 whole peppercorns
2 carrots, peeled and diced
24 button onions, peeled
75g/6tbsps frozen sweetcorn
140ml/¼ pint double cream
Salt and pepper

Cobbler Topping
400g/14oz plain flour
1½ tbsps baking powder
Pinch salt
75g/2½oz butter or margarine
Approximately 340ml/12fl oz milk
1 egg, beaten with a pinch of salt

1. Place the chicken in a deep saucepan with the water, bay leaf and peppercorns. Cover and bring to the boil. Reduce the heat and allow to simmer for 20-30 minutes, or until the chicken is tender. Remove the chicken from the pot and allow to cool. Skim and discard the fat from the surface of the stock. Skin the chicken and remove the meat from the bones.

2. Continue to simmer the stock until reduced by about half. Strain the stock and add the carrots and onions. Cook until tender and add the sweetcorn. Stir in the cream, add the chicken and season. Pour into a casserole or into individual baking dishes.

3. To prepare the topping, sift the dry ingredients into a bowl or place them in a food processor and process once or twice to sift.

4. Rub in the butter or margarine until the mixture resembles breadcrumbs. Stir in enough of the milk until the mixture comes together.

5. Turn out onto a floured surface and knead lightly. Roll out with a floured rolling pin to about 1.5cm/½ inch thick, and cut with a 5cm/2inch pastry cutter. Brush the surface of each round with a mixture of egg and salt. Place the rounds on top of the chicken mixture and bake for 10-15 minutes in a pre-heated oven at 190°C/375°F/Gas Mark 5. Serve immediately.

Step 4 Rub the butter or margarine into the dry ingredients until the mixture resembles breadcrumbs.

Step 5 Roll out the mixture on a floured surface, cut into rounds and place on top of the chicken mixture.

Cook's Notes

 Time
Preparation takes about 25 minutes and cooking takes 20-30 minutes for the chicken, about 20 minutes to prepare the sauce, and 10-15 minutes to finish off the dish.

 Preparation
Once the topping has been prepared it must be baked immediately or the baking powder will stop working and the cobbler topping will not rise.

 Variations
Diced potatoes and pimento may be added to the sauce along with other vegetables. Add chopped fresh parsley or a pinch of dried thyme as well, if wished.

SERVES 4

FRIED CHICKEN

Fried Chicken is easy to prepare and when it's home made, it's much better than a take away!

1.4kg/3lbs chicken portions
2 eggs
225g/8oz flour
1 tsp each salt, paprika and sage
½ tsp black pepper
Pinch cayenne pepper (optional)
Oil for frying
Parsley or watercress

Step 4 Coat the chicken on all sides with flour, shaking off the excess.

Step 2 Dip the chicken pieces in the egg to coat them well.

Step 6 Fry the chicken skin side first for 12 minutes, turn over and fry a further 12 minutes.

1. Rinse chicken and pat dry.

2 Beat the eggs in a large bowl and add the chicken one piece at a time, turning to coat.

3. Mix flour and seasonings in a large plastic bag.

4. Place chicken pieces coated with egg into the bag one at a time, close bag tightly and shake to coat each piece of chicken. Alternatively, dip each coated chicken piece in a bowl of seasoned flour, shaking off the excess.

5. Heat oil in a large frying pan to the depth of about 1.25cm/½ inch.

6. When the oil is hot, add the chicken skin side down first. Fry for about 12 minutes and then turn over. Fry a further 12 minutes or until the juices run clear.

7. Drain the chicken on kitchen paper and serve immediately. Garnish serving plate with parsley or watercress.

Cook's Notes

Time
Preparation takes about 20 minutes and cooking takes about 24 minutes.

Preparation
The chicken should not be crowded in the frying pan. If your pan is small, fry the chicken in several batches.

Cook's Tip
When coating anything for frying, be sure to coat it just before cooking. If left to stand, coating will usually become very soggy.

SERVES 4

CHICKEN ESCALOPES

There are a multitude of different methods of cooking
chicken, and this one although one of the simplest,
is also one of the most delicious.

4 boned and skinned chicken breasts
1 egg white
30g/8 tbsps wholemeal breadcrumbs
1 tbsp chopped fresh sage
Salt and freshly ground black pepper
2 tbsps walnut oil
120ml/4 fl oz mayonnaise
140ml/¼ pint natural unset yogurt
1 tsp grated fresh horseradish
2 tbsps chopped walnuts
Lemon slices and chopped walnuts to garnish

1. Pat the chicken breasts dry with kitchen paper.

2. Whisk the egg white with a fork until it just begins to
froth, but is still liquid.

3. Carefully brush all surfaces of the chicken breasts
with the beaten egg white.

4. Put the breadcrumbs onto a shallow plate and mix
in the chopped sage. Season with salt and freshly
ground black pepper.

5. Place the chicken breasts, one at a time, onto the
plate of breadcrumbs and sage, and carefully press this
mixture onto the surfaces of the chicken.

6. Put the oil into a large frying pan, and gently cook
the prepared chicken breasts on each side for 6-8
minutes until they are lightly golden and tender. Set
them aside, and keep warm.

7. Mix all the remaining ingredients, except for the
garnish, in a small bowl, whisking well to blend the
yogurt and mayonnaise evenly.

8. Place the cooked chicken breasts on a serving dish,
and spoon a little of the sauce over. Serve garnished
with the lemon slices and additional chopped nuts.

Step 2 Whisk the
egg white with a
fork until it
becomes frothy,
but still liquid.

Step 5 Press the
breadcrumb and
sage mixture onto
all surfaces of the
chicken breasts,
making sure that
they are covered
evenly.

Cook's Notes

 Time
Preparation takes about
20 minutes, cooking takes
12-16 minutes.

 Variation
Use almonds instead of
walnuts in this recipe, and
limes instead of lemons. Oranges
and hazelnuts make another
delicious variation.

 Serving Idea
Serve with lightly cooked
French beans and new
potatoes, or rice.

SERVES 6

COUNTRY CAPTAIN CHICKEN

A flavourful dish named after a sea captain
with a taste for the spicy cuisine of India.

1.4kg/3lbs chicken portions, skinned
Seasoned flour
90ml/6 tbsps oil
1 medium onion, chopped
1 medium green pepper, chopped
1 clove garlic, crushed
Pinch salt and pepper
2 tsps curry powder
2 x 400g/14oz cans tomatoes
2 tsps chopped fresh parsley
1 tsp chopped fresh marjoram
45g/4 tbsps currants or raisins
120g/4oz blanched almond halves

1. Dredge the chicken with flour, shaking off the excess.

2. Heat the oil in a large frying pan and brown the chicken on all sides until golden. Remove to an ovenproof casserole.

3. Pour off all but 2 tbsps of the oil. Add the onion, pepper and garlic and cook slowly to soften.

4. Add the seasoning and curry powder and cook, stirring frequently, for 2 minutes. Add the tomatoes, parsley and marjoram and bring to the boil. Pour the sauce over the chicken, cover and cook in a pre-heated oven to 180°C/350°F/Gas Mark 4 for 45 minutes. Add the currants or raisins during the last 15 minutes.

5. Meanwhile, toast the almonds in the oven on a baking sheet along with the chicken. Stir them frequently and watch carefully. Sprinkle over the chicken just before serving.

Step 4 Add the curry powder to the vegetables in the frying pan and cook for 2 minutes over low heat stirring frequently.

Step 4 Cook the remaining sauce ingredients and pour over the chicken.

Step 5 Toast the almonds on a baking sheet in the oven until light golden brown.

Cook's Notes

Time
Preparation takes about 30 minutes and cooking takes about 50 minutes.

Preparation
Country Captain Chicken can be prepared completely ahead of time and reheated for about 20 minutes in a moderate oven.

Serving Idea
If wished, serve the chicken with an accompaniment of boiled rice.

SERVES 4

CHICKEN WITH 'BURNT' PEPPERS AND CORIANDER

'Burning' peppers is a technique for removing the skins
which also imparts a delicious flavour to this favourite vegetable.

2 red peppers, halved lengthways and seeded
1 green pepper, halved lengthways and seeded
60ml/4 tbsps vegetable oil, for brushing
1 tbsp olive oil
2 tsps paprika
¼ tsp ground cumin
Pinch cayenne pepper
2 cloves garlic, crushed
460g/1lb canned tomatoes, drained and chopped
3 tbsps fresh chopped coriander
3 tbsps fresh chopped parsley
Salt, for seasoning
4 large, boned chicken breasts
1 large onion, sliced
60g/2oz flaked almonds

1. Put the peppers, cut side down, on a flat surface and gently press them with the palm of your hand to flatten them out.

2. Brush the skin side with 2 tbsps of the vegetable oil and cook them under a hot grill until the skin chars and splits.

3. Wrap the peppers in a clean towel for 10 minutes to cool.

4. Unwrap the peppers and carefully peel off the charred skin. Chop the pepper flesh into thin strips.

5. Heat the olive oil in a frying pan and gently fry the paprika, cumin, cayenne pepper and garlic for 2 minutes, stirring to prevent the garlic from browning.

6. Stir in the tomatoes, coriander, parsley and season with a little salt. Simmer for 15-20 minutes, or until thick. Set aside.

7. Heat the remaining vegetable oil in a flameproof dish, and sauté the chicken breasts, turning them frequently until they are golden brown on both sides.

8. Remove the chicken and set aside. Gently fry the onion in the oil for about 5 minutes, or until softened but not overcooked.

9. Return the chicken to the casserole with the onion and pour on about 280ml/½ pint of water. Bring to the boil.

10. Cover the casserole and simmer for about 30 minutes, turning the chicken occasionally to prevent it from burning.

11. Remove the chicken from the casserole and boil the remaining liquid rapidly to reduce to about 90ml/3 fl oz of stock.

12. Add the peppers and the tomato sauce to the chicken stock and stir well.

13. Return the chicken to the casserole, cover and simmer very gently for a further 30 minutes, or until the chicken is tender.

14. Arrange the chicken on a serving dish with a little of the sauce spooned over. Sprinkle with flaked almonds and serve any remaining sauce separately.

Cook's Notes

 Time
Preparation takes 30 minutes, cooking takes about 1 hour 30 minutes.

 Preparation
Take care not to cook this dish too rapidly or the peppers will disintegrate.

SERVES 4

CHICKEN AND CASHEW NUTS

Many oriental dishes are stir-fried. This simply means that
they are fried quickly in hot oil, the ingredients being stirred
continuously to prevent them from burning.

340g/12oz chicken breast, sliced into 2.5cm/1-inch
    pieces
1 tbsp cornflour
1 tsp salt
1 tsp sesame oil
1 tbsp light soy sauce
½ tsp sugar
75ml/5 tbsps vegetable oil
2 spring onions, trimmed and chopped
1 small onion, diced
2.5cm/1-inch piece fresh root ginger, peeled and
    finely sliced
2 cloves garlic, finely sliced
90g/3oz mange tout
60g/2oz bamboo shoots, thinly sliced
120g/4oz cashew nuts
2 tsps cornflour
1 tbsp hoisin sauce, or barbecue sauce
250ml/9 fl oz chicken stock

Step 2 Put the chicken pieces into the marinade mixture, and stir together well, to coat the pieces evenly.

Step 4 Add the mange tout and the bamboo shoots to the stir-fried onions in the wok, and continue stir-frying for about 3 minutes.

1. Roll the chicken pieces in the cornflour. Reserve any excess cornflour.

2. Mix together the salt, sesame oil, soy sauce and sugar in a large mixing bowl. Put the chicken into this marinade mixture and leave to stand in refrigerator for 10 minutes.

3. Heat 2 tbsps of the vegetable oil in a large wok and stir-fry the onions, ginger and garlic for 2-3 minutes.

4. Add the mange tout and the bamboo shoot to the onion mixture. Stir-fry for a further 3 minutes.

5. Remove the fried vegetables, add a further 1 tbsp oil to the wok and heat through.

6. Lift the chicken pieces out of the marinade and stir-

fry these in the hot oil for 3-4 minutes, until cooked through.

7. Remove the cooked chicken pieces and clean the wok.

8. Add the remaining oil and return the chicken and fried vegetables to the wok, and stir in the cashew nuts.

9. Mix together the 2 tsps of cornflour, plus the excess, with the hoisin or barbecue sauce and the chicken stock. Pour this over the chicken and vegetables in the wok and cook over a moderate heat, stirring continuously, until the ingredients are heated through and the sauce has thickened.

Cook's Notes

Time
Preparation takes about 15 minutes, and cooking takes about 15 minutes.

Variation
Stir 90g/3oz pineapple chunks into the stir-fry mixture just before serving.

Serving Idea
Serve this stir-fry with a dish of Chinese noodles.

SERVES 4-6

LEMON CHICKEN

Chicken, lemon and basil is an ideal flavour combination
and one that is used often in Greek cookery.

2 tbsps olive oil
30g/1oz butter or margarine
1 x 1.4kg/3lb chicken, jointed into 6-8 pieces
1 small onion, cut in thin strips
2 sticks celery, shredded
2 carrots, cut in julienne strips
1 tbsp chopped fresh basil
1 bay leaf
Juice and grated rind of 2 small lemons
140ml/¼ pint water
Salt and pepper
Pinch sugar (optional)
Lemon slices for garnishing

1. Heat the oil in a large frying pan. Add the butter or margarine and, when foaming, place in the chicken, skin side down, in one layer. Brown and turn over. Brown the other side. Cook the chicken in two batches if necessary. Remove the chicken to a plate and set aside.

2. Add the vegetables and cook 2-3 minutes over a moderate heat. Add the basil, bay leaf, lemon juice and rind, water, salt and pepper and replace the chicken. Bring the mixture to the boil.

3. Cover the pan and reduce the heat. Allow to simmer about 35-45 minutes or until the chicken is tender and the juices run clear when the thighs are pierced with a fork.

4. Remove the chicken and vegetables to a serving dish and discard the bay leaf. The sauce should be thick,

To cut the onion in thin strips, first cut in half through the root end. Using a sharp knife, follow the natural lines in the onion and cut through neatly to the flat base. Cut off the root end and the onion will fall apart in strips.

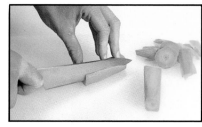

To make the carrots easier to cut into julienne strips, first cut them into rectangular blocks.

Cut the carrot blocks into thin slices and then stack them up to cut into strips quickly.

so boil to reduce if necessary. If the sauce is too tart, add a pinch of sugar. Spoon the sauce over the chicken to serve and garnish with lemon slices.

Cook's Notes

Time
Preparation takes about 30 minutes, cooking takes about 45-55 minutes total, including browning of chicken.

Variation
Use limes instead of lemons and oregano instead of basil.

Serving Idea
Pasta is often served with chicken dishes in Greece. Rice is also a good accompaniment, along with a green salad.

SERVES 4-6

CHICKEN WITH OLIVES

This is a chicken sauté dish for olive lovers.
Use more or less of them as your own taste dictates.

2 tbsps olive oil
30g/1oz butter or margarine
1 x 1.4kg/3lb chicken, jointed in 6-8 pieces
1 clove garlic, crushed
140ml/¼ pint white wine
140ml/¼ pint chicken stock
Salt and pepper
4 courgettes, cut in 1.25cm/½-inch pieces
20 pitted black and green olives
2 tbsps chopped parsley

1. Heat the oil in a large frying pan and add the butter or margarine. When foaming, add the chicken skin side down in one layer. Brown one side of the chicken and turn over to brown the other side. Cook the chicken in two batches if necessary.

To peel a garlic clove easily, first crush it gently with the side of a large knife. The skin will split, making it easier to remove.

To cut the courgettes quickly into chunks, first top and tail them, then cut them in half if small, or quarters if large, lengthwise. Gather the strips together and cut crosswise into chunks of the desired size.

Step 1 Cook the chicken, skin side down first, until golden brown.

2. Turn the chicken skin side up and add the garlic, wine, stock, salt and pepper. Bring to the boil, cover the pan and simmer over a gentle heat for about 30-35 minutes.
3. Add the courgettes and cook for 10 minutes. Once the chicken and courgettes are done, add the olives and cook to heat through. Add the parsley and remove to a dish to serve.

Cook's Notes

Time
Preparation takes about 25 minutes, cooking takes about 50-55 minutes.

Serving Idea
Serve with rice or pasta and tomato salad.

Variation
Artichoke hearts may be used in place of the courgettes.

SERVES 4-6

CHICKEN CACCIATORE

The name means Chicken the Hunter's Way,
and that means the addition of mushrooms.

3 tbsps oil
120g/4oz mushrooms, quartered, if large
1 x 1.4kg/3lb chicken, skinned if wished and cut into
   pieces
1 onion
2 cloves garlic
140ml/¼ pint vermouth
1 tbsp white wine vinegar
140ml/¼ pint chicken stock
460g/1lb canned tomatoes
1 tsp oregano
1 sprig fresh rosemary
Salt and pepper
60g/2oz black olives, pitted
2 tbsps chopped parsley

1. Heat the oil in a heavy-base frying pan and cook the mushrooms for about 1-2 minutes. Remove them and set aside. Brown the chicken in the oil and transfer the browned pieces to an ovenproof casserole.

2. Chop the onion and garlic finely. Pour off all but 1 tbsp of the oil in the frying pan and reheat the pan. Cook the onion and garlic until softened but not coloured. Add the vermouth and vinegar and boil to reduce by half. Add the chicken stock, tomatoes, oregano, rosemary, salt and pepper. Break up the tomatoes and bring the sauce to the boil. Allow to cook for 2 minutes.

3. Pour the sauce over the chicken in the casserole, cover and cook at 180°C/350°F/Gas Mark 4 for about 1 hour.

4. Add mushrooms and olives during the last 5 minutes of cooking.

5. Remove the rosemary before serving and sprinkle with chopped parsley.

Step 2 Cut onion in half lengthways leaving the root end intact. Holding the knife parallel to the chopping board, cut the onion in thin horizontal slices, but not through to the root end.

Step 2 Cut the onion lengthwise in thin strips, leaving the onion attached at the root end.

Step 2 Cut crosswise through the onion; the onion will fall apart into small dice.

Cook's Notes

Time
Preparation takes about 25-30 minutes and cooking takes about 1 hour 15 minutes.

Cook's Tip
Pitted black olives are available in most good supermarkets.

Serving Idea
Serve with spaghetti or pasta shapes and sprinkle with grated Parmesan cheese.

SERVES 6-8

COUNTRY CHICKEN STEW

Peppers, potatoes, sweetcorn, tomatoes, onions and
broad beans are staple ingredients in this recipe.

1.4kg/3lbs chicken portions
45g/6 tbsps flour
45g/1½oz butter or margarine
225g/8oz belly pork, rinded and cut into 5mm/¼ inch
   dice
3 medium onions, finely chopped
1.7ltrs/3 pints water
3 x 400g/14oz cans tomatoes
3 tbsps tomato purée
120g/4oz fresh or frozen broad beans
120g/4oz sweetcorn
2 large red peppers, cut into small dice
3 medium potatoes, peeled and cut into 1.25cm/
   ½ inch cubes
1-2 tsps cayenne pepper or Tabasco to taste
2 tsps Worcestershire sauce
280ml/½ pint red wine
Salt and pepper

1. Shake the pieces of chicken in the flour in a plastic bag to coat. In a large frying pan, melt the butter until foaming. Place in the chicken, without crowding the pieces, and brown over a moderately high heat for about 10-12 minutes. Remove the chicken and set it aside.

2. In the same pan, fry the belly pork until the fat is rendered and the dice are crisp.

3. Add the onions and cook over moderate heat for about 10 minutes, or until softened but not browned.

4. Pour the water into a large stock pot or saucepan and spoon in the onions, pork and any meat juices from the pan. Add the chicken, tomatoes and tomato purée. Bring to the boil, reduce the heat and simmer for about 1-1½ hours.

5. Add the broad beans, sweetcorn, peppers and potatoes. Add cayenne pepper or Tabasco to taste. Add the Worcestershire sauce and red wine. Season to taste.

6. Cook for a further 30 minutes or until the chicken is tender. Add salt and pepper to taste.

7. The stew should be rather thick, so if there is too much liquid, remove the chicken and vegetables and boil down the liquid to reduce it. If there is not enough liquid add more water or chicken stock.

Step 3 Add the onions and cook slowly until tender but not browned.

Step 4 Scrape the contents of the frying pan into a large stock pot or saucepan of water.

Cook's Notes

Time
Preparation takes about 1 hour and cooking takes about 2 hours.

Preparation
If wished, prepare the stew ahead of time, leaving out the last half hour of cooking. Bring slowly to the boil and then simmer for about 30 minutes more before serving.

Freezing
The stew may be frozen for up to 2 months in rigid containers. Cool the stew to room temperature before freezing.

SERVES 4

POULET FRICASSÉE

This is a white stew, enriched and thickened with an egg and cream mixture which is called a liaison in French cooking

60g/2oz butter
1 x 1.4kg/3lb chicken, quartered and skinned
30g/1oz flour
570ml/1 pint chicken stock
Juice and grated rind of ½ lemon
1 bouquet garni
12-16 small onions, peeled
340g/12oz button mushrooms, whole if small,
    quartered if large
2 egg yolks
90ml/6 tbsps double cream
3 tbsps milk (optional)
Salt and pepper
2 tbsps chopped parsley and thyme
Lemon slices to garnish

1. Melt 45g/1½oz of the butter in a large frying pan. Place in the chicken in one layer and cook over gentle heat for about 5 minutes, or until the chicken is no longer pink. Do not allow the chicken to brown. If necessary, cook the chicken in two batches. When the chicken is sufficiently cooked, remove it from the pan and set aside.

2. Stir the flour into the butter remaining in the pan and cook over very low heat, stirring continuously for about 1 minute, or until a pale straw colour. Remove the pan from the heat and gradually beat in the chicken stock. When blended smoothly, add lemon juice and rind, return the pan to the heat and bring to the boil, whisking constantly. Reduce the heat and allow the sauce to simmer for 1 minute.

3. Return the chicken to the pan with any juices that have accumulated and add the bouquet garni. The

Step 3 Tie a bay leaf, sprig of thyme and parsley stalks together to make a bouquet garni.

sauce should almost cover the chicken. If it does not, add more stock or water. Bring to the boil, cover the pan and reduce the heat. Allow the chicken to simmer gently for 30 minutes.

4. Meanwhile, melt the remaining butter in a small frying pan, add the onions, cover and cook very gently for 10 minutes. Do not allow the onions to brown. Remove the onions from the pan with a draining spoon and add to the chicken. Cook the mushrooms in the remaining butter for 2 minutes. Set the mushrooms aside and add them to the chicken 10 minutes before the end of cooking.

5. Test the chicken by piercing a thigh portion with a sharp knife. If the juices run clear, the chicken is cooked. Transfer chicken and vegetables to a serving plate and discard the bouquet garni. Skim the sauce of any fat and boil it rapidly to reduce by almost half.

6. Blend the egg yolks and cream together and whisk-in several spoonfuls of the hot sauce. Return the egg yolk and cream mixture to the remaining sauce and cook gently for 2-3 minutes. Stir the sauce constantly and do not allow it to boil. If very thick, add milk. Adjust the seasoning, stir in the parsley and thyme and spoon over the chicken in a serving dish. Garnish with lemon slices.

Cook's Notes

 Time
Preparation takes about 30 minutes, cooking takes about 30-40 minutes.

 Serving Idea
Serve with boiled potatoes or rice.

 Cook's Tip
Pour boiling water over the onions and leave to soak for 10 minutes to make them easier to peel.

 Watchpoint
A fricassée is a white stew. Cook gently to avoid browning the ingredients.

SERVES 4

SIMPLE CHICKEN CASSEROLE

This is really a cheat's recipe – a can of soup saves a
great deal of time, but the end result is delicious.

1 tbsp oil
30g/1oz butter
8 chicken thighs
280g/10oz can condensed cream of mushroom soup
225g/8oz button mushrooms, sliced
3 tbsps single cream
60ml/4 tbsps dry sherry

1. Heat the oil and butter in a heavy-based frying pan,
add the chicken pieces skin side down and cook until
golden brown, then turn them and brown the other side.

2. Mix the can of soup, the sliced mushrooms, cream
and sherry.

3. Place the chicken in an ovenproof dish or casserole
and pour the sauce over. Cover and bake in an oven
preheated to 190°C/375°F/Gas Mark 5 for 1¼-1½ hours
or until the chicken is tender.

Step 1 Sauté the
chicken pieces on
both sides until
golden brown.

Step 2 Mix the
soup, mushrooms,
cream and sherry
together.

Cook's Notes

 Time
Preparation takes about 10
minutes and cooking takes
about 1¼-1½ hours.

 Variation
You can add shallots to the
sauce for more flavour.

 Serving Idea
Serve with sautéed potatoes
or rice and French beans.

SERVES 4

CHICKEN WITH CORIANDER AND PILAU RICE

Exotic spices used to be a frequent accompaniment to chicken dishes, and this dish combines a wide selection of spices.

2 tbsps oil
30g/1oz butter
8 chicken thighs
1 large onion, sliced
1 tsp paprika
1 tsp cumin powder
1 tsp turmeric
½ tsp dried thyme
Freshly ground black pepper
280ml/½ pint well-flavoured chicken stock
30g/1oz pitted black olives (about 10 olives)
2 tbsps finely chopped fresh coriander
Squeeze lemon juice

For the Pilau Rice
45g/1½oz butter
60g/2oz whole blanched almonds
1 small onion, finely diced
60g/2oz sultanas or raisins
340g/12oz long grain rice
700ml/1¼ pints boiling water
½ tsp salt

1. Heat the oil and butter in a large frying pan and sauté the chicken until an even golden brown colour. Transfer to a plate.

2. Add the onion to the remaining fat and sauté until softened and tinged with brown.

3. Add the paprika, cumin and turmeric and cook for 1 minute. Add the thyme, black pepper and stock and bring to the boil.

4. Return the chicken to the pan, skin side down. Cover and simmer for 40-45 minutes or until tender.

5. Remove the chicken with a slotted spoon to a warm serving dish and keep warm.

6. Reduce the sauce by boiling rapidly until it thickens. Stir in the olives, coriander and lemon juice, season to taste and spoon over the chicken.

Step 6 Stir the olives, coriander and lemon juice into the thickened sauce.

7. To prepare the pilau rice, melt 15g/½oz of the butter in a small pan and when hot add the almonds and fry until lightly tinged with brown.

8. Dip the base of the pan into cold water to cool it down and prevent further cooking.

9. Melt the remaining butter in large saucepan and fry the onion over a gentle heat until softened, but not coloured.

10. Add the fried almonds, sultanas and rice and fry for 1 minute. Add the boiling water and salt. Bring to the boil. Cover, reduce the heat to low and simmer for 15 minutes, until all the water has been absorbed.

11. Fork the rice lightly and serve with the chicken.

Cook's Notes

Time
Preparation takes about 20 minutes and cooking takes 40-45 minutes.

Serving Idea
A chilled white wine from Alsace complements this dish well.

Preparation
Prepare the pilau rice while the chicken is cooking, so they are both ready to serve at the same time.

SERVES 4

CHICKEN WITH SAFFRON RICE AND PEAS

Saffron gives rice and sauces a lovely golden colour and delicate taste.

2 tbsps oil
1 x 1kg/2¼lb chicken, cut into 8 pieces and skinned if
   wished
Salt and pepper
1 small onion, finely chopped
2 tsps paprika
1 clove garlic, crushed
8 tomatoes, skinned, seeded and chopped
275g/10oz rice
700ml/1¼ pints boiling water
Large pinch saffron or ¼ tsp ground saffron
175g/6oz frozen peas
2 tbsps chopped parsley

1. Heat the oil in a large frying pan. Season the chicken with salt and pepper and place it in the hot oil, skin side down first. Cook over moderate heat, turning the chicken frequently to brown it lightly. Set the chicken aside.

2. Add the onions to the oil and cook slowly until softened but not coloured.

3. Add the paprika and cook for about 2 minutes, stirring frequently until the paprika loses some of its red colour. Add the garlic and the tomatoes.

4. Cook the mixture over high heat for about 5 minutes to evaporate the liquid from the tomatoes. The mixture should be of dropping consistency when done. Add the rice, water and saffron and stir together.

5. Return the chicken to the casserole and bring to the boil over a high heat. Reduce to simmering, cover tightly and cook for about 20 minutes. Remove the chicken and add the peas and parsley. Cook a further 5-10 minutes, or until the rice is tender. Combine with the chicken to serve.

Step 3 Add the paprika and cook until it loses some of its red colour.

Step 4 When the garlic and tomatoes are added, cook over a high heat to evaporate the liquid until the mixture is of a dropping consistency.

Step 5 Stir in the peas and parsley and cook for five minutes.

Cook's Notes

Time
Preparation takes about 20-25 minutes and cooking takes about 25-35 minutes.

Variation
If using fresh peas, allow about 400g/14oz of peas in their pods. Cook fresh peas with the rice and chicken.

Serving Idea
This is a very casual, peasant-type dish which is traditionally served in the casserole in which it was cooked.

SERVES 4

POACHED CHICKEN WITH CREAM SAUCE

Plainly cooked chicken can be as flavourful as it is attractive.

1 x 2kg/4½lb chicken
8-10 celery sticks, washed, cut into 7.5cm/3-inch
  lengths and tops reserved
120g/4oz thickly sliced streaky bacon
2 cloves garlic, crushed
1 large onion, stuck with 4 cloves
1 bay leaf
1 sprig fresh thyme
Salt and pepper
Water to cover
90g/3oz butter or margarine
45g/6 tbsps flour
280ml/½ pint single cream

1. Tie the chicken legs together, then place in a large casserole or stock pot. Chop the celery tops and add to the pot. Place the bacon over the chicken and add the garlic, onion with the cloves, bay leaf, sprig thyme, salt, pepper and water to cover.

2. Bring to the boil, reduce the heat and simmer gently, covered, for 50 minutes or until the chicken is just tender. Add the celery and simmer a further 20 minutes, or until the celery is just tender.

3. Remove the chicken to a serving plate and keep warm. Strain the stock and reserve the bacon and celery pieces. Skim fat off the top of the stock and add enough water to make up 570ml/1 pint, if necessary.

4. Melt 15g/½oz of the butter or margarine in the casserole and sauté the bacon until just crisp. Drain on kitchen paper and crumble roughly.

5. Melt the rest of the butter in the casserole and when foaming take off the heat. Stir in the flour and gradually add the chicken stock. Bring to the boil, stirring constantly. Add the cream and simmer until the mixture is thickened.

6. Untie the legs and trim leg ends. If wished, remove the skin from the chicken before coating with the sauce. Garnish with the bacon and the reserved celery pieces.

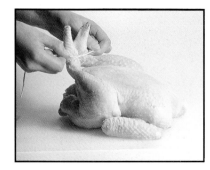

Step 1 Tie the legs together but do not cross them over.

Step 1 Arrange the bacon over the chicken, add the celery tops and the rest of the ingredients.

Cook's Notes

 Time
Preparation takes about 20 minutes and cooking takes about 1 hour 10 minutes.

 Serving Idea
The chicken may be jointed into 8 pieces before coating with sauce, if wished. Cut the leg joint in two, dividing the thigh and the drumstick. Cut the breast in two, leaving some white meat attached to the wings. Cut though any bones with scissors.

 Variation
Sliced or whole baby carrots may be added with the celery. Small onions may also be cooked with the celery.

SERVES 6

TOMATO AND BACON FRIED CHICKEN

Not the usual crisp fried chicken, this is cooked in
a tomato sauce flavoured with garlic, herbs and wine.

Flour for dredging
Salt and pepper
1 x 1.4kg/3lb chicken, cut into serving pieces
90ml/6 tbsps oil
75g/2½oz butter or margarine
1 clove garlic, crushed
1 small onion, finely chopped
120g/4oz streaky bacon or green gammon, diced
6 tomatoes, skinned and chopped
2 tsps fresh thyme or 1 tsp dried thyme
Salt and pepper
140ml/¼ pint white wine
2 tbsps chopped parsley

1. Mix the flour with salt and pepper and dredge the chicken lightly, shaking to remove any excess flour. Heat the oil in a large frying pan and, when hot, add the butter.

2. Add the chicken drumstick and thigh pieces skin side down and allow to brown. Turn the pieces over and brown on the other side. Brown over moderately low heat so that the chicken cooks as well as browns. Push the chicken to one side of the pan, add the breast meat, and brown in the same way.

3. Add the garlic, onion and bacon or gammon to the pan and lower the heat. Cook slowly for about 10 minutes, or until the bacon browns slightly. Add the tomatoes and thyme and lower the heat. Cook until the chicken is just tender and the tomatoes are softened.

4. Using a draining spoon, transfer the chicken and other ingredients to a serving dish and keep warm. Remove all but about 60ml/4 tbsps of the fat from the pan and deglaze with the wine, scraping up the browned bits from the bottom. Bring to the boil and allow to reduce slightly. Pour over the chicken to serve, and sprinkle with chopped parsley.

Step 1 Dredge the chicken very lightly with flour and shake to remove the excess.

Step 2 Brown all the chicken on both sides slowly, until golden.

Cook's Notes

Time
Preparation takes about 25 minutes and cooking takes about 30-40 minutes.

Preparation
Brown the chicken slowly so that it cooks at the same time as it browns. This will cut down on the length of cooking time needed once all the ingredients are added.

Variation
Add finely chopped green or red pepper or celery along with the onion and garlic. If more sauce is preferred, use one 400g/14oz can of tomatoes and juice. Substitute chicken stock for the wine.

SERVES 6

CHICKEN WITH CLOUD EARS

Cloud ears is the delightful name for an edible tree
fungus which is mushroom-like in taste and texture.

12 cloud ears, wood ears or other dried Chinese
  mushrooms, soaked in boiling water for 10 minutes
460g/1lb skinned and boned chicken breasts, thinly sliced
1 egg white
2 tsps cornflour
2 tsps white wine
2 tsps sesame oil
280ml/½ pint oil for deep-frying
2.5 cm/1-inch piece fresh root ginger, left whole
1 clove garlic
280ml/½ pint chicken stock
1 tbsp cornflour
3 tbsps light soy sauce
Pinch salt and pepper

1. Soak the mushrooms until they soften and swell. Mix the chicken with the egg white, cornflour, wine and sesame oil.

2. Heat the wok for a few minutes and pour in the oil for deep-frying. Add the whole piece of ginger and whole garlic clove to the oil and cook for about 1 minute. Take them out and reduce the heat.

3. Add about a quarter of the chicken at a time and stir-fry for about 1 minute. Remove and continue cooking until all the chicken is fried. Remove all but about 2 tbsps of the oil from the wok.

4. Drain the mushrooms and squeeze them to extract all the liquid. If using mushrooms with stems, remove the stems before slicing thinly. Cut cloud ears or wood ears into smaller pieces. Add to the wok and cook for about 1 minute.

5. Add the stock and allow it to come almost to the boil. Mix together the cornflour and soy sauce and add a spoonful of the hot stock. Add the mixture to the wok, stirring constantly, and bring to the boil. Allow to boil for 1-2 minutes or until thickened. The sauce will clear when the cornflour has cooked sufficiently.

6. Return the chicken to the wok and add salt and pepper. Stir thoroughly for about 1 minute and serve immediately.

Step 1 Soak the cloud ears or mushrooms in boiling water for 10 minutes, they will swell in size.

Step 3 Stir-fry the chicken in small batches, placing in the oil with chopsticks.

Cook's Notes

 Time
Preparation takes about 25 minutes, cooking takes about 5 minutes.

 Preparation
If wished the chicken may be cut into 2.5cm/1 inch cubes. If slicing, cut across the grain as this helps the chicken to cook more evenly.

 Buying Guide
Dried cloud ears or wood ears are available from Chinese supermarkets and some delicatessens. Shiitake mushrooms are more readily available. Both keep a long time in their dried state.

SERVES 4

CHICKEN POLISH STYLE

Choose small, young chickens for a truly Polish
style dish. A dried white roll was originally
used for stuffing, but breadcrumbs are easier.

2 x 900g/2lb chickens
15g/½ oz butter or margarine
2 chicken livers
6 slices bread, made into crumbs
1 egg
2 tsps chopped parsley
1 tsp chopped dill
Salt and pepper
140ml/¼ pint chicken stock

1. Remove the fat from just inside the cavities of the
chicken and discard it. Melt the butter in a small frying
pan. Pick over the chicken livers and cut away any
discoloured portions. Add chicken livers to the butter
and cook until just brown. Chop and set aside.

2. Combine the breadcrumbs, egg, herbs, salt and
pepper and mix well. (Chopped mushrooms or onions
may be added to the stuffing, if wished.) Mix in the
chopped chicken livers.

3. Stuff the cavities of the chickens and sew up the

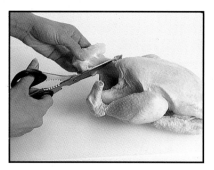

Step 1 Remove
the fat from the
inside of the cavity
of each chicken
and discard it.

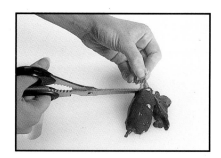

Step 1 Pick over
the chicken livers
and remove any
discoloured parts.

Step 3 Fill the
chickens and sew
up the opening
with fine thread
using a trussing
needle.

openings with fine thread using a trussing needle. Tie
the legs together.

4. Place the chickens in a roasting tin and spread the
breasts and legs lightly with more butter. Pour the stock
around the chickens and roast in a preheated 190°C/
375°F/Gas Mark 5 oven for about 55-60 minutes. Baste
frequently with the juices during roasting.

5. When the chickens are done, remove them from the
roasting tin, and keep them warm. Remove the string.
Skim any fat from the surface of the pan juices. If a lot
of liquid has accumulated, pour into a small saucepan
and reduce over high heat. Pour the juices over the
chickens to serve.

Cook's Notes

Time
Preparation takes about 20
minutes and cooking takes
about 55-60 minutes.

Cook's Tip
To check if chicken is
cooked, pierce thickest part
of thigh with a skewer. Juices should
run clear.

Serving Idea
Serve with a cucumber salad
or a Polish style lettuce salad
and new potatoes tossed with butter
and dill.

CHAPTER 4

NICE & SPICY

SERVES 6

SPICY SPANISH CHICKEN

Chillies, coriander and sunny tomatoes add
warm Spanish flavour to grilled chicken.

6 boned chicken breasts
Grated rind and juice of 1 lime
2 tbsps olive oil
Coarsely ground black pepper
90ml/6 tbsps whole grain mustard
2 tsps paprika
4 ripe tomatoes, skinned, seeded and quartered
2 shallots, chopped
1 clove garlic, crushed
½ Jalapeno pepper or other chilli, seeded and chopped
1 tsp wine vinegar
Pinch salt
2 tbsps chopped fresh coriander
Whole coriander leaves to garnish

1. Place chicken breasts in a shallow dish with the lime rind and juice, oil, pepper, mustard and paprika. Marinate for about 1 hour, turning occasionally.

2. To skin tomatoes easily, drop them into boiling water for about 20 seconds or less depending on ripeness. Place immediately in cold water. Skins should come off easily.

3. Place the tomatoes, shallots, garlic, chilli, vinegar and salt in a food processor and process until coarsely chopped. Stir in the coriander by hand.

4. Place chicken on a grill pan and reserve the marinade. Grill chicken skin side uppermost for about 7-10 minutes, depending on how close the chicken is to the heat source. Baste frequently with the remaining marinade. Grill other side in the same way. Sprinkle with salt after grilling.

5. Place chicken on serving plates and garnish top with coriander leaves or sprigs. Serve with a spoonful of the tomato relish on one side.

Step 1 Marinate chicken in a shallow dish, turning occasionally to coat.

Step 2 Tomatoes skin easily when placed first in boiling water and then in cold.

Step 4 Grill skin side of chicken until brown and crisp before turning pieces over.

Cook's Notes

Time
Preparation takes about 1 hour including marinating and cooking takes 14-20 minutes.

Preparation
Tomato relish can be prepared in advance and kept in the refrigerator.

Watchpoint
When preparing chillies, wear rubber gloves or at least be sure to wash hands thoroughly after handling them. Do not touch eyes or face before washing hands.

SERVES 4-6

CHICKEN, SAUSAGE AND OKRA STEW

There is an exotic taste to this economical chicken stew.
The garlic sausage adds flavour instantly.

120ml/4fl oz oil
1 x 1.4kg/3lb chicken, cut into 6-8 pieces
120g/4oz flour
1 large onion, finely chopped
1 large green pepper, roughly chopped
3 sticks celery, finely chopped
2 cloves garlic, crushed
225g/8oz garlic sausage, diced
1150ml/2 pints chicken stock
1 bay leaf
Dash Tabasco
Salt and pepper
120g/4oz fresh okra

1. Heat the oil in a large frying pan and brown the chicken on both sides, 3-4 pieces at a time. Transfer the chicken to a plate and set it aside.

2. Lower the heat under the pan and add the flour. Cook over a very low heat for about 30 minutes, stirring constantly until the flour turns a rich, dark brown. Take the pan off the heat occasionally, so that the flour does not burn.

3. Add the onion, green pepper, celery, garlic and sausage to the pan and cook for about 5 minutes over a very low heat, stirring continuously.

4. Pour on the stock and stir well. Add the bay leaf, a dash of Tabasco, salt and pepper. Return the chicken to the pan, cover and cook for about 30 minutes or until the chicken is tender.

5. Top and tail the okra and cut each into 2-3 pieces. If okra are small, leave whole. Add to chicken and cook for a further 10-15 minutes. Remove the bay leaf and serve.

Step 2 Continue cooking over low heat, stirring constantly as the flour begins to brown.

Step 3 When the flour is rich dark brown, add the remaining sauce ingredients.

Cook's Notes

Time
Preparation takes about 30 minutes and cooking takes about 1 hour 25 minutes.

Cook's Tip
The oil and flour roux may be made ahead of time and kept in the refrigerator to use whenever needed. If the roux is cold, heat the liquid before adding.

Serving Idea
Serve on a bed of rice.

SERVES 4

AUBERGINE AND CHICKEN CHILLI

This unusual dish is both delicious and filling.

2 medium-sized aubergines
60ml/4 tbsps sesame oil
2 cloves garlic, crushed
4 spring onions
1 green chilli, finely chopped
340g/12oz boned and skinned chicken breast
60ml/4 tbsps light soy sauce
2 tbsps stock, or water
1 tbsp tomato purée
1 tsp cornflour
Sugar to taste

1. Cut the aubergine into quarters lengthways, using a sharp knife. Slice the aubergine quarters into pieces approximately 1.25cm/½-inch thick.

2. Put the aubergine slices into a bowl and sprinkle liberally with salt. Stir well to coat evenly. Cover with cling film and leave to stand for 30 minutes.

3. Rinse the aubergine slices very thoroughly under running water, then pat dry with a clean tea cloth.

4. Heat half of the oil in a wok, or large frying pan, and gently cook the garlic until it is soft, but not coloured.

5. Add the aubergine slices to the wok and cook, stirring frequently, for 3-4 minutes.

6. Using a sharp knife, slice the spring onions into thin

Step 6 Cut the spring onions diagonally into small pieces, aproximately 1.25 cm/½-inch long.

diagonal strips. Stir the spring onions together with the chilli into the cooked aubergine, and cook for a further 1 minute. Remove the aubergine and onion from the pan, and set aside, keeping warm.

7. Cut the chicken breast into thin slices with a sharp knife.

8. Heat the remaining oil in the wok, and fry the chicken pieces for approximately 2 minutes or until they have turned white and are thoroughly cooked.

9. Return the aubergine and onions to the pan and cook, stirring continuously, for 2 minutes or until heated through completely.

10. Mix together the remaining ingredients and pour these over the chicken and aubergines in the wok, stirring constantly until the sauce has thickened and cleared. Serve immediately.

Cook's Notes

Time
Preparation takes about 10 minutes plus 30 minutes standing time. Cooking takes about 15 minutes.

Cook's Tip
The vegetables can be prepared well in advance, but the aubergines should be removed from the salt after 30 minutes, or they will become too dehydrated.

Serving Idea
Serve this recipe as part of a more extensive Chinese style meal.

SERVES 4

SPICY CHICKEN

This is a really aromatic dish, perfect
for special midweek dinner parties.

4 large dry red chillies
½ tsp cumin seed
¼ tsp fennel seed
2 tbsps coriander seed
2.5cm/1-inch fresh ginger, peeled and roughly chopped
1 clove garlic, roughly chopped
Juice 1 lime
8 chicken thighs or drumsticks, skinned and boned
Salt
2 tbsps oil

Step 1 Soak the dried chillies in boiling water for 5 minutes.

1. Soak the chillies in boiling water for 5 minutes.

2. Meanwhile, put the cumin seed, fennel seed and coriander seed into a dry frying pan and roast over a high heat shaking the pan, until the seeds become slightly coloured and give off a spicy aroma.

3. Drain the chillies and put them, with the dry roasted spices, ginger and garlic, into a food processor, coffee grinder, or pestle and mortar and grind to a paste. Then gradually add the lime juice.

4. Cut the chicken into 2.5cm/1-inch cubes, stir in the chilli paste and a pinch of salt.

5. Leave to marinate in the fridge for 2 hours.

6. Heat the oil in a large frying pan and sauté the chicken pieces over a medium heat for 15-20 minutes until firm to the touch and cooked through. Do not be tempted to overcrowd the pan – they should only be cooked in a single layer. If necessary, cook in batches and keep warm. Serve immediately.

Step 3 Grind the chillies, the dry roasted spices, ginger and garlic to a paste.

Step 6 Sauté the chicken pieces over a medium heat for 15-20 minutes or until cooked through. Do not overcrowd the pan.

Cook's Notes

Time
Preparation takes about 15 minutes, plus 2 hours marinating time. Cooking takes about 20 minutes.

Serving Idea
Serve with a salad of chopped tomatoes, cucumbers and carrot on a bed of lettuce, with thick yogurt on the side.

Cook's Tip
Toasting the whole spices helps to develop their flavour.

CHICKEN MOGHLAI WITH CORIANDER CHUTNEY

The creamy spiciness of the chicken is a good
contrast to the hotness of the chutney.

60ml/4 tbsps oil
1.4kg/3lbs chicken pieces, skinned
1 tsp ground cardamom
½ tsp ground cinnamon
1 bay leaf
4 cloves
2 onions, finely chopped
2.5cm/1-inch piece fresh root ginger, grated
4 cloves garlic, crushed
30g/1oz ground almonds
2 tsps cumin seeds
Pinch cayenne pepper
280ml/½ pint single cream
90ml/6 tbsps natural yogurt
2 tbsps roasted cashew nuts
2 tbsps sultanas
Salt

Chutney
90g/3oz fresh coriander leaves
1 green chilli, seeded and chopped
1 tbsp lemon juice
Salt and pepper
Pinch sugar
1 tbsp oil
½ tsp ground coriander

1. To prepare the chicken, heat the oil in a large frying pan. Fry the chicken pieces on each side until golden brown.

2. Remove the chicken and set aside. Put the cardamom, cinnamon, bay leaf and cloves into the hot oil and meat

Step 7 Stir the yogurt, cashews and sultanas into the chicken. Heat through gently to plump up the sultanas, but do not allow the mixture to boil.

juices and fry for 30 seconds. Stir in the onions and fry until soft but not brown.

3. Stir the ginger, garlic, almonds, cumin and cayenne pepper into the onions. Cook gently for 2-3 minutes, then stir in the cream.

4. Return the chicken pieces to the pan, along with any juices. Cover and simmer gently for 30-40 minutes, or until the chicken is cooked and tender.

5. Whilst the chicken is cooking, prepare the chutney: Put the coriander leaves, chilli, lemon, seasoning and sugar into a blender or food processor and work to a paste.

6. Heat the oil and cook the ground coriander for 1 minute. Add this mixture to the processed coriander leaves and blend in thoroughly.

7. Just before serving, stir the yogurt, cashews and sultanas into the chicken. Heat through just enough to plump up the sultanas, but do not allow the mixture to boil.

8. Serve at once with the coriander chutney.

Cook's Notes

Time
Preparation takes about 25 minutes, and cooking takes 30-40 minutes.

Preparation
The coriander chutney can be prepared using a pestle and mortar, if a blender or food processor is not available.

Serving Idea
Serve with boiled rice and a cucumber and tomato salad.

SERVES 4-6

CHICKEN TOMATO

Made with a very fragrant selection of spices,
this dish is sure to become a firm favourite.

.1 onion, chopped
3 tbsps oil
2.5cm/1-inch piece cinnamon stick
1 bay leaf
6 cloves
Seeds of 6 small cardamoms
2.5cm/1-inch piece fresh root ginger, grated
4 cloves garlic, crushed
1 x 1.4kg/3lb chicken, cut into 8-10 pieces
1 tsp chilli powder
1 tsp ground cumin
1 tsp ground coriander
1 x 400g/14oz can tomatoes, chopped
1 tsp salt
2 sprigs fresh coriander leaves, chopped
2 green chillies, halved and seeded

1. In a large saucepan, fry the onion in the oil, until it has softened. Add the cinnamon, bay leaf, cloves, cardamom seeds, ginger and garlic. Cook for 1 minute.

2. Add the chicken pieces to the saucepan. Sprinkle the chilli powder, ground cumin and coriander over the chicken in the pan. Fry for a further 2 minutes, stirring continuously, to ensure the spices do not burn.

Step 2 Fry the chicken and spices together, stirring continuously, to prevent the spices burning.

Step 3 Mix the canned tomatoes and remaining seasonings into the chicken, stirring thoroughly to blend the spices evenly.

3. Stir in the remaining ingredients, mixing well to blend the spices evenly. Cover the pan and simmer for 40-45 minutes, or until the chicken is tender.

Cook's Notes

Time
Preparation takes about 30 minutes, and cooking takes about 40-50 minutes.

Serving Idea
Serve with boiled rice.

SERVES 4-6

CHICKEN TIKKA

Red food colouring gives this dish its
traditional appearance, but the taste will not
be affected if you prefer not to use it.

140ml/¼ pint natural yogurt
1 tsp chilli powder
2 tsps ginger paste
2 tsps garlic paste
2 tsps garam masala
½ tsp salt
¼ tsp red food colouring
Juice of 1 lemon
1 x 1.4kg/3lb chicken, cut into 8-10 pieces
Oil for brushing

Step 2 Add the chicken pieces to the yogurt mixture, stirring well, to make sure thay are evenly coated.

Step 1 In a large bowl, mix together the yogurt, chilli powder, ginger and garlic pastes, garam masala, salt, colouring and lemon juice.

Step 3 Line a grill pan with aluminium foil and arrange the chicken pieces on this.

1. In a large bowl, mix together the yogurt, chilli powder, ginger and garlic pastes, garam masala, salt, colouring and lemon juice.

2. Add the chicken pieces to the yogurt mixture and mix well to ensure they are evenly coated. Cover and refrigerate for at least 2 hours.

3. Line a grill pan with aluminium foil and arrange the chicken pieces on this, together with the yogurt sauce. Preheat the grill to moderate and grill the chicken pieces for about 8-10 minutes on each side, brushing with a little oil if necessary, to prevent them burning.

Cook's Notes

Time
Preparation takes about 10 minutes plus 2 hours marinating and cooking takes about 16-20 minutes.

Variation
Use chicken drumsticks instead of a whole cut chicken.

Preparation
Chicken can be marinated overnight if wished.

SERVES 6

FLAUTAS

Traditionally, these are long, thin rolls of tortillas with
savoury fillings, topped with sour cream.

225g/8oz chicken, skinned, boned and minced or
  finely chopped
1 tbsp oil
1 small onion, finely chopped
½ green pepper, finely chopped
½-1 chilli, seeded and finely chopped
90g/3oz frozen sweetcorn
6 black olives, pitted and chopped
120ml/4 fl oz double cream
Salt
12 prepared tortillas
Taco sauce, guacamole and sour cream for toppings.

1. Use a food processor or meat mincer to prepare the
chicken, or chop by hand.

2. Heat the oil in a medium frying pan and add the
chicken, onion and green pepper. Cook over moderate
heat, stirring frequently to break up the pieces of chicken.

3. When the chicken is cooked and the vegetables are
softened, add the chilli, sweetcorn, olives, cream and
salt. Bring to the boil over heat and boil rapidly, stirring
continuously, to reduce and thicken the cream.

4. Place 2 tortillas on a clean work surface, overlapping
them by about 5cm/2 inches. Spoon some of the chicken
mixture onto the tortillas, roll up and secure with cocktail
sticks.

5. Fry the flautas in about 1.25cm/½ inch oil in a large
frying pan. Do not allow the tortillas to get very brown.
Drain on kitchen paper.

6. Arrange the flautas on serving plates and top with
sour cream, guacamole and taco sauce.

Step 4 Place
tortillas slightly
overlapping on
work surface and
fill with chicken.

Step 4 Use
cocktail sticks to
secure tortillas.

Step 5 Fry slowly
and turn carefully
so the filling does
not leak.

Cook's Notes

 Time
Preparation takes about 15
minutes and cooking takes
about 15 minutes.

 Variation
Green olives, may be
substituted for black, and red
peppers for green.

 Serving Idea
Flautas are often served with
rice, refried beans and a
salad.

SERVES 4

SPICY BARBECUE CHICKEN

Whether you cook this recipe in the oven on a cold winter's evening or on the barbecue in the height of summer, it is bound to be a success.

4 chicken portions
140ml/¼ pint maple syrup or clear honey
¼ tsp cayenne pepper
½ tsp salt
Freshly ground black pepper
2 cloves garlic, crushed
2 tbsps tomato purée
1 tbsp Dijon mustard
2 tbsps lemon juice

Step 3 Spoon enough of the sauce over the chicken to coat each joint well.

Step 1 Lay the chicken joints in a roasting tin, skinned side uppermost.

1. Skin the chicken joints and lay them in a roasting tin, skinned side uppermost.

2. Meanwhile, mix together the remaining ingredients to make the barbecue sauce.

3. Spoon enough sauce over the chicken to coat each joint well.

4. Bake in a oven preheated to 230°C/450°F/Gas Mark 8 for 30-40 minutes, basting the chicken once or twice with the sauce.

5. Test the chicken, in the thickest part, with a sharp knife. If the juices run clear it is cooked, if the juices are pink then return the chicken to the oven for another 5-10 minutes and test again. Serve the extra sauce separately.

Cook's Notes

Time
Preparation takes about 10 minutes, cooking takes about 30-40 minutes.

Variation
You can use this sauce when cooking chicken portions on the barbecue. It is a good idea to marinate the chicken in the sauce for at least 4 hours before you start the barbecue, to get a really good flavour.

Serving Idea
Serve with jacket potatoes and either a green salad or a selection of seasonal vegetables.

SERVES 4

CHICKEN IN RED PEPPER SAUCE

This recipe blends the exotic spices of the
Far East with the delicate flavour of chicken.

4 large boneless chicken breasts, skinned
30g/1oz butter
1 tbsp oil
1 medium onion, roughly chopped
2.5cm/1-inch fresh ginger, peeled
3 cloves garlic
30g/1oz blanched almonds
340g/12oz red pepper, roughly chopped
1 tbsp cumin powder
2 tsps coriander powder
1 tsp turmeric powder
Pinch cayenne pepper
½ tsp salt
90ml/6 tbsps vegetable oil
140ml/¼ pint water
3 star anise
2 tbsps lemon juice
Freshly ground black pepper

1. Cut the chicken breasts into largish pieces about 5cm/2 inches long and 2.5cm/1inch wide.

2. Heat the butter and oil in a frying pan, add the chicken pieces and cook for 5 minutes. Remove to a plate.

3. Combine the onion, ginger, garlic, almonds, red pepper, cumin, coriander, turmeric, cayenne and salt in a food processor or liquidizer.

4. Blend to a smooth paste. Heat the oil in a large saucepan or deep frying pan. Add the paste and fry for 10-12 minutes.

5. Add the chicken pieces, the water, star anise, lemon juice and black pepper. Cover, reduce the heat and simmer gently for 20-25 minutes, or until the chicken is tender. Stir a few times during cooking.

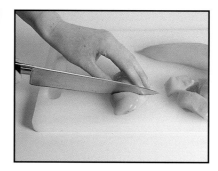

Step 1 Cut the chicken breasts into largish pieces.

Step 4 Blend onion, ginger, garlic, almonds, red peppers, cumin, coriander, turmeric, cayenne and salt to a smooth paste.

Step 5 Add chicken pieces, water, star anise, lemon juice and black pepper to the pan.

Cook's Notes

 Time
Preparation takes about 30 minutes and cooking takes about 25 minutes.

 Serving Idea
Serve with plain boiled or pilau rice.

 Buying Guide
Star anise is available from Oriental stores and some large supermarkets. If not available, substitute ¼ tsp of Chinese five-spice or fennel seeds.

SERVES 4

AROMATIC CHICKEN CURRY

This isn't quite what you'd expect from a curry, for it is not hot,
yet such voluptuous flavours are more representative of Indian
cooking than dishes which burn the roof of your mouth off.

225g/8oz onion, finely chopped
1 tbsp granulated sugar
8 whole, unpeeled garlic cloves
1 fresh lime, quartered
1 cinnamon stick
8 cardamom pods
6 whole cloves
2 sachets powdered saffron, or to taste
8 chicken thighs, skinned
570ml/1 pint boiling water
120g/4oz creamed coconut
Salt and freshly ground black pepper
2-3 bananas, peeled and cut into large chunks

1. Cook the onion in a little oil or butter until very soft, then
sprinkle over the sugar and cook over a moderate heat
until it has caramelised and the onions are golden brown.

2. Add the garlic, lime, cinnamon stick, cardamom,
cloves and saffron, stir well, then place the chicken
pieces in the pan and pour over the water.

3. Bring to the boil, cover and simmer gently until the
chicken is tender – about 30 minutes.

4. Remove the chicken and keep warm. Ideally you should
take out the lime, cinnamon stick and the other whole
spices.

5. Break up the creamed coconut and gradually stir the
pieces into the liquid, taking care not to let it boil.

Step 1 Cook the
onion in a little oil
or butter until very
soft. Add the sugar
and cook until
caramelised.

Step 5 Gradually
stir in the broken-
up creamed
coconut then cook
gently and do not
boil.

6. Taste and adjust the seasoning – add extra coconut
if you like a thicker or richer sauce, but be careful not
to hide the subtle taste of the spices.

7. Return the chicken pieces to the sauce with the
pieces of banana. Warm gently for a few minutes then
serve.

Cook's Notes

Time
Preparation takes about 20
minutes and cooking takes
about 40 minutes.

Variation
If you cannot find saffron but
like the yellow colour, you
can substitute turmeric, although it
will not give quite the same flavour.

Serving Idea
Serve with lightly fried cashew
nuts, mango chutney or
natural yogurt with cucumber and
mint.

SERVES 6

SPECIAL OCCASION CURRIED CHICKEN

This recipe makes a delicious alternative to plain roasted chicken and will appeal to the whole family.

1 x 1.6kg/3½lb chicken
45g/1½oz butter
1 onion, finely chopped
2 cloves garlic, crushed
2.5cm/1-inch fresh root ginger, peeled and finely grated
3 tbsps curry powder
1 small green chilli, de-seeded and finely chopped
420ml/¾ pint chicken stock
3 tbsps mango chutney
1 tbsp soft brown sugar
Juice of ½ lemon
Good pinch garam masala
Boiled rice, to serve

1. Put the chicken in a deep roasting dish or casserole which has a tight-fitting lid.

2. Heat the butter in a saucepan and sauté the onion and garlic over a gentle heat until soft.

3. Add the ginger, curry powder and chopped chilli and

Step 2 Sauté the onion and garlic over a gentle heat until soft.

Step 3 Add the stock, mango chutney, sugar and lemon juice, and simmer uncovered for 30 minutes.

Step 4 Pour the sauce over the chicken and cook for 2½ hours, basting occasionally with the juices in the dish.

cook for 2 minutes. Add the stock, mango chutney, sugar and lemon juice and simmer, uncovered, for 30 minutes.

4. Pour this sauce over the chicken, cover and cook in an oven preheated to 160°C/325°F/Gas Mark 3 for 2½ hours, basting the chicken occasionally with the juices in the dish. Then remove the lid and return to the oven for a further 30 minutes to allow the sauce to evaporate and thicken.

5. Sprinkle with garam masala and serve with boiled rice.

Cook's Notes

Time
Preparation takes about 10 minutes and cooking takes about 3½ hours.

Variation
You can substitute a few drops of chilli sauce for the fresh chilli.

Serving Idea
As an alternative to boiled rice, serve with naan bread, and perhaps a spicy sambal, or chutney.

CHAPTER 5

ENTERTAINING

SERVES 2

HOT CHICKEN WITH PEACHES

Tangy with fresh ginger and fruit vinegar, this combination
makes a delicious summer dinner party dish.

340g/12oz boneless chicken meat
2 tbsps fruit vinegar (or cider vinegar)
1 tbsp finely grated fresh root ginger
340-460g/12oz-1lb fresh peaches
2 tbsps oil
2 tbsps dry white wine
1 tbsp sliced fresh mint
Salt and freshly ground black pepper

1. If using breast meat, cut into 3 or 4 long, thin strips.
If using thigh or drumstick meat, keep in large pieces.

2. Put the chicken into a shallow dish with the fruit or
cider vinegar and the grated ginger, cover and leave
to marinate in a cool place for a few hours.

3. Meanwhile, drop the peaches into boiling water for
2 minutes, then peel and cut into segments.

4. Drain the marinade from the chicken and reserve.

5. Heat the oil in a large frying pan, then add the chicken

and cook over medium heat for 5-7 minutes, turning
from time to time, until cooked through.

6. Remove the chicken to a warm dish. Pour the marinade
and the wine into the pan, season and, when hot, slide
in the peaches and heat through without stirring.

7. Sprinkle the mint leaves into this hot liquid and the
moment they have wilted, remove the pan from the heat.
Serve the chicken topped with the peaches and with the
hot vinaigrette strained over the combination.

Step 3 Drop the
peaches into
boiling water for 2
minutes, then peel
and cut into
segments.

Step 2 Put the
sliced chicken into
a shallow dish to
marinate with the
vinegar and
ginger.

Step 5 Sauté the
chicken in a large
frying pan for 5-7
minutes or until
cooked through.

Cook's Notes

Time
Preparation takes about 30
minutes, plus a minimum of 2
hours marinating time. Cooking
takes about 15 minutes.

Variation
If you like a more savoury
flavour, soften an ounce of
very finely chopped onion and/or a
little garlic in the oil before adding the
chicken, but do not let either burn.

Serving Idea
Serve this dish on top of a
mixed salad, or accompanied
by a selection of plainly cooked,
seasonal vegetables.

SERVES 4

POULET SAUTÉ VALLÉE D'AUGE

This dish contains all the ingredients that Normandy
is famous for – butter, cream, apples and Calvados.

60g/2oz butter or margarine
2 tbsps oil
1 x 1.4kg/3lb chicken, jointed into eight pieces
60ml/4 tbsps Calvados
90ml/6 tbsps chicken stock
2 dessert apples, peeled, cored and coarsely chopped
1 shallot, finely chopped
2 sticks celery, finely chopped
½ tsp dried thyme, crumbled
2 egg yolks, lightly beaten
90ml/6 tbsps double cream
Salt and pepper

Garnish

30g/1oz butter
2 dessert apples, quartered, cored and cut into cubes
Sugar
1 bunch watercress or small parsley sprigs

Step 1 Brown the chicken a few pieces at a time, skin side down first.

Step 7 Cook diced apple until it begins to caramelise.

1. Melt half the butter and all of the oil in a large frying pan over moderate heat. When the foam begins to subside, brown the chicken, a few pieces at a time, skin side down first. When all the chicken is browned, pour off most of the fat from the pan and return the chicken to the pan.

2. Pour the Calvados into the pan and warm over gentle heat. Ignite with a match, shake the pan gently until the flames subside.

3. Pour over the stock and scrape up any browned chicken juices from the bottom of the pan. Set the chicken aside.

4. Melt the remaining butter in a small saucepan or frying pan. Cook the chopped apples, shallot and celery and the thyme for about 10 minutes or until soft but not brown.

5. Spoon over the chicken and return the pan to the high heat. Bring to the boil, then reduce heat, cover the pan and simmer for 50 minutes.

6. When the chicken is cooked, beat the eggs and cream together. With a whisk, gradually beat in some of the hot sauce. Pour the mixture back into a saucepan and cook over a low heat for 2-3 minutes, stirring constantly until the sauce thickens and coats the back of a spoon. Season to taste and set aside while preparing the garnish.

7. Put the butter in a small frying pan and when foaming, add the apple. Toss over a high heat until beginning to soften. Sprinkle with sugar and cook until the apple begins to caramelise.

8. To serve, coat the chicken with the sauce and decorate with watercress or parsley. Spoon the caramelised apples over the chicken.

Cook's Notes

 Time
Preparation takes 25-20 minutes, cooking takes 55-60 minutes.

 Watchpoint
Do not allow the sauce to boil once the egg and cream is added or it will curdle.

 Serving Idea
Serve with sauté potatoes and fresh young peas.

SERVES 4-6

VENETIAN CHICKEN

This elegant dinner party dish incorporates traditional Italian ingredients.
It is a delicious recipe which can't fail to impress your guests.

1 tbsp olive oil
30g/1oz butter
1 onion, finely sliced
2 cloves garlic, crushed
460g/1lb boneless chicken breasts, skinned and cut
    into 1.2cm/½-inch cubes
1 tsp dried oregano
225g/8oz Italian risotto rice
1 tbsp tomato purée
1150ml/2 pints good chicken stock
Splash white wine
Salt and freshly ground black pepper
6 tomatoes, skinned, de-seeded and chopped
10 pitted black olives, halved
2 tbsps chopped parsley
60g/2oz Parmesan cheese, grated

1. Heat the oil and butter in a large frying pan and sauté the onion and garlic over a gentle heat until soft and lightly browned.

2. Add the diced chicken and cook until pale brown. Add the oregano and rice and cook for 1 minute until the rice is transparent, then add the tomato purée, stock and wine.

3. Season with salt and pepper and stir well. Do not be tempted to stir again during cooking, since this would make the rice sticky.

4. Cook over a very gentle heat for about 25-30 minutes, until all the stock has been absorbed but the rice still has a slight bite to it.

5. Lightly fork in the tomatoes, olives and chopped parsley, cook for 2 minutes and served sprinkled with Parmesan cheese.

Step 1 Sauté the onion and garlic over a gentle heat until soft and lightly browned.

Step 2 Add the diced chicken and sauté until lightly browned.

Step 5 Lightly fork in the tomatoes, olives and chopped parsley. Cook for 2 minutes.

Cook's Notes

 Time
Preparation takes about 15 minutes and cooking takes about 30 minutes.

Variation
If you prefer, you can substitute a can of tomatoes, drained and chopped, for the six fresh tomatoes.

 Serving Idea
Serve with a chilled white wine – Frascati complements this dish very well. Accompany with a mixed green salad.

SERVES 4

CHICKEN WITH BLACKCURRANT SAUCE

The sharp tang of blackcurrants makes an ideal
partner for lightly cooked chicken.

4 boned and skinned chicken breasts
3 tbsps sesame oil
225g/8oz fresh blackcurrants
Juice of 1 orange
140ml/¼ pint red wine
Sugar to taste
Orange slices and fresh blackcurrants to garnish

1. Season the chicken breasts with a little salt. Heat the oil in a shallow frying pan.

Step 2 Gently fry the chicken breasts in the hot oil until they are golden brown on all sides.

2. Gently fry the chicken breasts for 6-8 minutes on each side, until they are golden brown and tender.

3. Meanwhile, put the blackcurrants into a small pan, along with the orange juice and red wine. Bring to the boil, then cover and simmer gently until the blackcurrants are soft.

4. Using a liquidiser or food processor, blend the blackcurrants and the cooking juice for 30 seconds.

5. Rub the blended purée through a fine nylon sieve with

Step 5 Press the blackcurrant purée through a fine nylon sieve with a wooden spoon, to remove all the pips and skins.

Step 6 Simmer the sieved fruit purée until it has thickened and the liquid has reduced.

the back of a spoon, pressing the fruit through to reserve all the juice and pulp but leaving the pips in the sieve.

6. Put the sieved purée into a small saucepan and heat gently, stirring constantly until the liquid has reduced and the sauce is thick and smooth, adding a little sugar to sweeten if necessary.

7. Arrange the chicken breasts on a serving dish, and spoon the blackcurrant sauce over. Garnish with orange slices and fresh blackcurrants.

Cook's Notes

 Time
Preparation takes 15 minutes, cooking takes approximately 20 minutes.

 Preparation
To test if the chicken breasts are cooked, insert a skewer into the thickest part, then press gently, if the juices run clear, the meat is cooked.

 Variation
Use blackberries instead of blackcurrants in this recipe.

SERVES 4

ROAST CHICKEN WITH GARLIC AND HERB SAUCE

This dinner party dish is extremely impressive and yet very easy.

1 medium lemon
1 large and 1 small Boursin cheese with garlic and herbs
1 x 1.4kg/3lb chicken
2 small bay leaves

1. Grate the lemon zest directly into a small bowl and mash up all the large Boursin evenly with this.

2. Ease this mixture evenly and gently between the breast and the skin of the bird.

Step 2 Ease the soft cheese under the skin of the chicken to cover the breast meat in an even layer.

3. Put the bay leaves into the chicken cavity and put the chicken into a roasting bag or enclose in foil.

4. Squeeze the lemon and pour the juice into the bag; put the lemon halves into the cavity of the chicken.

5. Seal and slash roasting bag as directed and bake at 190°C/375°F/Gas Mark 5 for 20 minutes per 460g/1lb, plus 20 minutes extra.

6. Cut the bag and pour all the juices, including those inside the chicken, into a measuring jug.

Step 6 Pour all the meat juices into a measuring jug.

7. Now carefully pour away the fat which will have risen to the top until you have about 140ml/¼ pint of well-flavoured stock, reheat gently and then remove from heat.

8. Chop the small Boursin into pieces and whisk into the warm sauce. Carve the chicken and pour on the sauce immediately.

Step 8 Cut up the small Boursin and whisk the pieces into the warm sauce.

Cook's Notes

 Time
Preparation takes about 20 minutes and cooking takes about 1 hour 20 minutes.

 Serving Idea
A chilled rosé wine from Provence is an excellent accompaniment to this dish.

 Variation
You could try ringing the changes by using pepper-flavoured Boursin or by combining two flavours, using one for the stuffing and one for the sauce.

SERVES 4

POUSSINS WITH DEVILLED SAUCE

Although this recipe takes quite a while to prepare,
the end result will make your effort worthwhile.

4 single (small) poussins
1 tsp each of paprika, mustard powder and ground
  ginger
½ tsp ground turmeric
¼ tsp ground allspice
60g/2oz butter
2 tbsps chilli sauce
1 tbsp plum chutney
1 tbsp brown sauce
1 tbsps Worcestershire sauce
1 tbsp soy sauce
Dash Tabasco sauce
3 tbsps chicken stock

1. Tie the legs of each poussin together.

2. Put the paprika, mustard and ginger, turmeric and allspice, into a small bowl and mix together well.

3. Rub the spice mixture evenly all over the poussins, pushing some behind the wings and into the joints, then refrigerate them for at least 1 hour.

4. Arrange the poussins in a roasting tin. Melt the butter and brush it evenly over the birds. Roast, for 20 minutes, in an oven preheated to 180°C/350°F/Gas Mark 4 brushing with the roasting juices during this time.

5. Put the chilli sauce, plum chutney, brown sauce, Worcestershire sauce, soy sauce, Tabasco and chicken stock into a small bowl and mix well.

6. Brush about half of this sauce over the poussins. Return to the oven and cook for a further 20-30 minutes.

7. Brush the poussins twice more with the remaining sauce mixture during this final cooking time so that the skins become brown and crisp.

Step 1 Tie the legs of each poussin together with trussing thread.

Step 3 Rub the poussins all over with the spice mixture, pressing it down into the wings and joints.

Cook's Notes

 Time
Preparation takes about 20 minutes, plus 1 hour standing time. Cooking takes 40-50 minutes, depending on the size of the poussins.

 Serving Idea
Serve with fresh cooked pasta and a large salad.

Cook's Tip
The poussins could be refrigerated overnight with the spices.

SERVES 4

LIME ROASTED CHICKEN

Roast chicken, cooked with the tangy flavour
of limes makes the perfect summer meal.

4 chicken breast portions, each weighing about
  225g/8oz
Salt and fresh ground black pepper
4 limes
2 tsps white wine vinegar
75ml/5 tbsps olive oil
2 tsps fresh chopped basil

1. Rub chicken portions all over with salt and black pepper. Place in a shallow ovenproof dish, and set aside.

2. Remove the zest from 2 of the limes, using a zester. Cut these 2 limes in half and squeeze the juice.

3. Add lime juice to the vinegar and 60ml/4 tbsps of the olive oil in a small dish, along with the zest and mix well.

4. Pour the oil and lime juice mixture over the chicken portions in the dish. Cover and refrigerate for about 4 hours or overnight.

5. Remove the covering from the dish in which the chicken is marinating, and baste the chicken well with the marinade mixture. Place into an oven preheated to 190°C/375°F/Gas Mark 5 and cook for 30-35 minutes, or until the chicken is well roasted and tender.

6. In the meantime, cut off all the rind and white pith from the remaining 2 limes with a sharp knife, and cut the limes into thin slices.

7. Heat the remaining oil in a small frying pan and add the lime slices and basil. Cook quickly for 1 minute, or until the fragrance rises up from the basil and the limes just begin to soften.

8. Serve the chicken portions on a serving platter, garnished with the fried lime slices and a little extra fresh basil, if wished.

Step 5 After marinating for 4 hours, the chicken portions will look slightly cooked and the meat will have turned a pale opaque colour.

Step 7 Fry the lime slices very quickly in the hot oil until they just begin to soften.

Cook's Notes

 Time
Preparation takes 25 minutes, plus at least 4 hours marinating time. Cooking takes 40 minutes.

 Preparation
The chicken can be prepared in advance and marinated overnight.

 Variation
Use lemons instead of limes, and thyme instead of basil.

 Watchpoint
Allow the chicken about 30 minutes to come to room temperature before cooking.

SERVES 4

CHICKEN WITH WALNUTS & CELERY

Oyster sauce lends a subtle, slightly salty taste to this Cantonese dish.

225g/8oz boned chicken, cut into 2.5cm/1-inch pieces
2 tsps soy sauce
2 tsps brandy
1 tsp cornflour
Salt and pepper
2 tbsps oil
1 clove garlic
120g/4oz walnut halves
3 sticks celery
2 tsps oyster sauce
140ml/¼ pint water or chicken stock

Step 3 Add the walnuts to the wok and cook until they are crisp.

Step 4 Use a large, sharp knife to cut the celery on the diagonal into thin slices.

Step 3 Cook the chicken until done but not brown.

1. Combine the chicken with the soy sauce, brandy, cornflour, salt and pepper.

2. Heat a wok and add the oil and garlic. Cook for about 1 minute to flavour the oil.

3. Remove the garlic and add the chicken in two batches. Stir-fry quickly without allowing the chicken to brown. Remove the chicken and add the walnuts to the wok. Cook for about 2 minutes until the walnuts are slightly brown and crisp.

4. Slice the celery diagonally, add to wok and cook for about 1 minute. Add the oyster sauce and water and bring to the boil. When boiling, return the chicken to the pan and stir to coat all the ingredients well. Serve immediately.

Cook's Notes

 Time
Preparation takes about 20 minutes, cooking takes about 8 minutes.

! Watchpoint
Nuts can burn very easily. Stir them constantly for even browning.

Variation
Almonds or cashew nuts may be used instead of the walnuts. Add along with the celery.

SERVES 4

MARINATED CHICKEN WITH WALNUT SAUCE

Offer your guests a walnut sauce that tastes delicious and is very easy to make.

2 x 900g/2lb chickens cut in half

Marinade
140ml/¼ pint olive oil
Juice and grated rind of 2 lemons
1 tbsp chopped fresh oregano
Pinch ground cumin
1 tbsp chopped fresh parsley
2 tsps chopped fresh thyme
Salt and pepper
Pinch sugar

Walnut Sauce
2 cloves garlic, roughly chopped
4 slices bread, crusts removed, soaked in water for 10 minutes
2 tbsps white wine vinegar
60-75ml/4-5 tbsps olive oil
1-2 tbsps water (optional)
Salt and pepper
90g/3oz ground walnuts

1. Remove the backbones from the chickens with poultry shears. Bend the legs backwards to break the ball and socket joint. Cut away some of the ribcage with a sharp knife. Flatten the chickens slightly with a meat mallet or rolling pin. Mix together the marinating ingredients in a large, shallow dish or a large plastic bag. Place in the chickens and turn to coat. If using a plastic bag, fasten securely and place in a dish to catch any drips. Refrigerate for at least 4 hours or overnight.

2. Place the chickens on a grill pan and cook under low

Step 1 Remove the backbone from the chickens using a pair of sharp poultry shears or a cleaver.

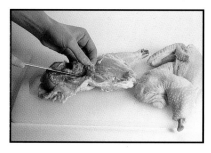

Step 1 Cut away some of the ribcage to make the chickens easier to flatten with a meat mallet or rolling pin.

heat for about 30 minutes, turning and basting frequently with the marinade. Raise the heat and cook for a further 10 minutes, skin side up, to brown nicely.

3. Meanwhile, place the garlic in a food processor and squeeze the bread to remove the water. Add the bread to the food processor along with the vinegar. With the machine running, pour the oil through the funnel in a thin, steady stream. Add water if necessary to bring the sauce to coating consistency. Add salt and pepper and stir in the walnuts by hand. When the chicken is cooked, remove to a serving dish and pour over any remaining marinade. Serve with the walnut sauce.

Cook's Notes

Time
Preparation takes 30 minutes, plus at least 4 hours marinating time, cooking takes about 40 minutes.

Cook's Tip
If grill does not have an adjustable setting, pre-cook the chicken in the oven for about 30 minutes and then grill for the remaining time until done.

Serving Idea
Garnish with lemon wedges and sprigs of parsley or other fresh herbs, if wished. Serve with rice and a green or tomato salad.

SERVES 4

CHICKEN WITH RED PEPPERS

Easy as this recipe is, it looks and
tastes good enough for any guests.

4 large red peppers
4 skinned and boned chicken breasts
1½ tbsps oil
Salt and pepper
1 clove garlic, finely chopped
3 tbsps white wine vinegar
2 spring onions, finely chopped
Sage leaves for garnish

Step 1 Flatten the peppers with the palm of the hand and brush them with oil.

1. Cut the peppers in half lengthwise, and remove the stems, cores and seeds. Flatten the peppers with the palm of your hand and brush the skin sides lightly with some oil.

2. Place the peppers skin side up on the rack of a pre-heated grill and cook about 5cm/2 inches away from the heat source until the skins are well blistered and charred.

3. Wrap the peppers in a clean towel and allow them to stand until cool. Peel off the skins with a small vegetable knife. Cut peppers into thin strips and set aside.

4. Place the chicken breasts between two sheets of dampened greaseproof paper and flatten by hitting with a rolling pin or meat mallet.

5. Heat the oil in a large frying pan. Season the chicken breasts on both sides and place in the hot oil. Cook for 5 minutes, turn over and cook until tender and lightly browned. Remove the chicken and keep it warm.

6. Add the pepper strips, garlic, vinegar and spring onions to the pan and cook briefly until the vinegar loses its strong aroma.

7. Place the chicken breasts on serving plates. Spoon over the pan juices.

8. Arrange the pepper mixture with the chicken and garnish with the sage leaves.

Step 2 Cook the peppers until the skins are blistered and well charred.

Step 3 Peel off the skins using a small vegetable knife.

Cook's Notes

Time
Preparation takes about 35-40 minutes and cooking takes about 10 minutes to char the peppers and about 20 minutes to finish the dish.

Variation
For convenience, the dish may be prepared with canned pimento caps instead of red peppers. These will be softer so cook the garlic, vinegar and onions to soften, and then add pimento.

Buying Guide
If fresh sage is unavailable, substitute coriander or parsley leaves as a garnish.

SERVES 4

COQ AU VIN

Originating from the Burgundy region this dish is probably the most famous chicken recipe in all of France. It is very rich, definitely a cold weather meal.

225g/8oz thick cut streaky bacon
420ml/¾ pint water
12-16 button onions or shallots
30g/1oz butter or margarine
225g/8oz mushrooms, left whole if small, quartered if large
1 x 1.4kg/3lb chicken, jointed in eight pieces
420ml/¾ pint dry red wine
3 tbsps brandy
1 bouquet garni
1 clove garlic, crushed
3 tbsps flour
420ml/¾ pint chicken stock
Salt and pepper
4 slices bread, crusts removed
Oil for frying
2 tbsps chopped parsley

1. Cut the bacon into strips about 5mm/¼-inch thick. Bring water to the boil and blanch the bacon by simmering for 5 minutes. Remove the bacon with a draining spoon and dry on kitchen paper. Re-boil the water and drop in the onions. Allow them to boil rapidly for 2-3 minutes and then plunge into cold water and peel. Set the onions aside with the bacon.

2. Melt half the butter in a large frying pan over moderate heat and add the bacon and onions. Sauté over high heat, stirring frequently and shaking the pan, until the bacon and onions are golden brown. Remove them with a draining spoon and leave on kitchen paper. Add the remaining butter to the saucepan and cook the mushrooms for 1-2 minutes. Remove them and set aside with the onions and bacon.

3. Reheat the frying pan and brown the chicken, a few pieces at a time. When all the chicken is browned, transfer it to a large ovenproof casserole.

Step 1 Cut the bacon into small strips and blanch to remove excess salt.

4. Pour the wine into a small saucepan and boil to reduce to about 280ml/½ pint. Pour the brandy over the chicken and warm over a low heat. Ignite with a match and shake the casserole carefully until the flames die down. Add the bouquet garni and garlic to the casserole.

5. Pour off all but 1 tbsp of fat from the frying pan and stir in the flour. Cook over gentle heat, scraping up any of the browned chicken juices from the bottom of the pan. Stir in the reduced wine and add the stock. Bring the sauce to the boil over high heat, stirring constantly until thickened. Strain over the chicken in the casserole and cover tightly.

6. Place in an oven preheated to 180°C/350°F/Gas Mark 4, and cook for 20 minutes. After that time, add the bacon, onions and mushrooms and continue cooking for a further 15-20 minutes, or until the chicken is tender. Remove the bouquet garni and season with salt and pepper.

7. Cut each of the bread slices into 4 triangles. Heat enough oil in a large frying pan to cover the triangles of bread. When the oil is very hot, add the bread triangles two at a time and fry until golden brown and crisp. Drain on kitchen paper. To serve, arrange the chicken in a deep dish, pour over the sauce and vegetables and arrange the fried bread croûtes around the outside of the dish. Sprinkle with chopped parsley.

Cook's Notes

Time
Preparation takes 30-40 minutes, cooking takes about 50 minutes.

Watchpoint
Make sure the oil for frying the croûtes is hot enough when the bread is added, otherwise croûtes can be very oily.

Cook's Tip
Blanching the bacon in boiling water removes excess saltiness. Boiling the onions makes them easier to peel.

SERVES 4

SPRING CHICKEN WITH BITTER CHOCOLATE SAUCE

Unsweetened chocolate lends a delightfully mysterious flavour to a savoury sauce.

60ml/4 tbsps olive oil
4 single (small) poussins
Salt and pepper
3 tbsps flour
1 clove garlic, crushed
280ml/½ pint chicken stock
60ml/4 tbsps dry white wine
2 tsps unsweetened cooking chocolate, grated
Lemon slices to garnish

Step 2 Cook the flour in the oil until it turns a pale straw colour.

Step 1 Brown the poussins in the hot oil, turning carefully to avoid tearing the skin.

Step 5 Stir the grated chocolate into the sauce and cook over low heat to melt it.

1. Heat the oil in a heavy-based pan or casserole. Season the poussins and place them, breast side down first, in the hot oil. Cook until golden brown on all sides, turning frequently.

2. Transfer the poussins to a plate and add flour to the casserole. Cook to a pale straw colour.

3. Add the garlic and cook to soften. Pour on the stock gradually, mixing well. Add the wine and bring to the boil.

4. Reduce to simmering, replace the poussins and cover the casserole. Cook 30-40 minutes, or until the poussins are tender.

5. Transfer the cooked poussins to a serving dish and skim any fat from the surface of the sauce. Add the grated chocolate and cook, stirring quickly, over low heat for 2-3 minutes. Pour some of the sauce over the poussins and garnish with lemon slices. Serve the rest of the sauce separately.

Cook's Notes

Time
Preparation takes about 20 minutes, cooking takes about 35-45 minutes.

Buying Guide
Unsweetened cooking chocolate is not the same as plain chocolate, which must not be used as a substitute. Unsweetened chocolate is available in large supermarkets and speciality shops.

Serving Idea
Serve with rice and a vegetable such as peas or asparagus, or with a green salad.

SERVES 4

SPATCHCOCKED POUSSINS IN MUSTARD

This is a very eye-catching dish and very simple to prepare.

2 double (large) poussins (each about 675g/1½lbs in weight)
120g/4oz butter, softened
2 tbsps wholegrain mustard
2 tsps sugar
Salt and freshly ground black pepper
Bunch watercress to garnish

1. To 'spatchcock' the poussins, turn each one over and cut through flesh and bone from tail to neck along one side of the backbone. Then flip over so that the skin side is uppermost.

2. Open the bird out flat and press along the breastbone with the heel of the hand to flatten it thoroughly.

3. Lay the birds bony side uppermost and grill for 7-10 minutes.

4. Meanwhile, mix the butter with the mustard and sugar. Turn the birds over and spread with the mustard butter.

5. Season with salt and pepper and grill for another 10-12 minutes, or until cooked through and deep brown. To serve, cut the poussins in half along the breast bones, and garnish with watercress.

Step 2 Open the poussins out flat, skin side up, and flatten the breast bone with the heel of the hand.

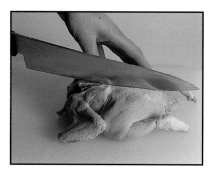

Step 1 Turn each poussin upside down and cut in half from tail to neck along one side of the backbone.

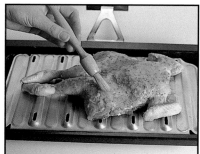

Step 4 Brush the skin side of the poussins with the butter, mustard and sugar glaze.

Cook's Notes

Time
Preparation takes about 20 minutes and cooking takes about 20 minutes.

Cook's Tip
The poussins can be threaded onto long skewers to help turning over when grilling.

Serving Idea
A chilled, light white wine goes very well with this dish.

SERVES 4

CHICKEN IN MUSTARD AND BRANDY SAUCE

This dish is a real dinner party dazzler.
It tastes delicious and doesn't take long to prepare.

30g/1oz butter
8 chicken thighs
5 large garlic cloves, unpeeled
75ml/5 tbsps wine vinegar
280ml/½ pint dry white wine
2 tbsps brandy
2 tsps Dijon mustard
1 heaped tsp tomato purée
280ml/½ pint double cream
2 tomatoes, skinned and de-seeded

Step 1 Brown chicken on both sides and add unpeeled garlic cloves.

Step 8 Sieve the sauce into the cream, pressing the garlic well.

1. Heat the butter in a large, heavy-based frying pan. Fry the chicken thighs on both sides to brown them evenly. Add the unpeeled garlic cloves and reduce the heat.

2. Cover the pan and cook gently for 20 minutes, or until the chicken is tender.

3. Pour out all but 1 tbsp of fat from the pan and add the vinegar, stirring well and scraping up any browned juices from the bottom.

4. Boil rapidly until the liquid is reduced to about 2 tablespoons.

5. Lift out the chicken and keep warm.

6. Add the wine, brandy, mustard and tomato purée to the pan. Mix well and boil rapidly for 5 minutes or until reduced to a thick sauce.

7. In another heavy saucepan, boil the cream until reduced by half, stirring frequently to prevent it burning. Take off the heat.

8. Sieve the vinegar sauce into the cream, pressing the garlic cloves well to remove the pulp. Season with salt and black pepper.

9. Cut the de-seeded tomatoes into thin strips and stir into the sauce. Reheat the sauce if necessary.

10. Arrange the chicken on a hot serving dish and spoon over the sauce to serve.

Cook's Notes

Time
Preparation takes about 25 minutes and cooking takes about 30 minutes.

Variation
If you prefer, chicken breasts can be used rather than thighs.

Serving Ideas
Serve with new or sautéed potatoes and courgettes.

SERVES 6

CHICKEN WITH CHERRIES

Canned cherries make an easy
sauce that really dresses up chicken.

60ml/4 tbsps oil
6 chicken breasts, skinned and boned
1 sprig fresh rosemary
Grated rind and juice of ½ lemon
140ml/¼ pint red wine
Salt and pepper
460g/1lb canned black cherries, pitted
2 tsps cornflour

Step 1 Cook the chicken breasts until just lightly browned. Watch carefully, as skinned chicken will dry out easily.

1. Heat the oil in a frying pan over a moderate heat. Place in the chicken breasts, skinned side down first. Cook until just lightly browned. Turn over and cook the second side for about 2 minutes.

2. Remove any oil remaining in the pan and add the rosemary, lemon rind, wine and salt and pepper. Bring to the boil and then lower the heat.

3. Add the cherries and their juice. Cook, covered, for 15 minutes or until the chicken is tender. Remove the chicken and cherries and keep them warm. Discard the rosemary.

4. Mix the cornflour and lemon juice. Add several spoonfuls of the hot sauce to the cornflour mixture. Return the mixture to the frying pan and bring to the boil, stirring constantly, until thickened and cleared.

5. Pour sauce over the chicken and cherries. Heat through and serve.

Cook's Notes

Time
Preparation takes about 10 minutes and cooking takes about 20 minutes.

Preparation
Serve the chicken dish on the day that it is cooked – it does not keep well.

Serving Idea
Serve with rice, and accompany with a green vegetable such as lightly steamed mange tout.

SERVES 4

TOMATO POUSSINS WITH CORIANDER

A wonderful combination of flavours makes
this an excellent dinner party dish.

4 single (small) poussins
1 sachet powdered saffron
225g/8oz can tomatoes, whole or chopped
30g/1oz fresh coriander, leaves and stalks
2 large cloves garlic
60g/2oz butter
Salt and fresh ground black pepper

Step 2 Paint the poussins all over with the saffron mixture.

Step 1 Trim off any loose skin, and cut the parson's noses from the poussins.

Step 3 Put most of the roughly chopped coriander into the cavities of the poussins.

1. Trim the birds of any loose skin and parson's noses.

2. Dissolve the saffron in a little of the juice from the tomatoes and paint the birds all over with this. Take care when handling saffron, as it stains – ideally, wear a pair of rubber gloves.

3. Fold the coriander a few times, chop roughly and put most of it into the cavities of the birds.

4. Put the birds into a baking dish with just large enough to accommodate them, with the tomatoes.

5. Crush the garlic over them, then dot with butter and sprinkle with the remaining coriander.

6. Season lightly with salt and pepper, turn the birds onto their sides and cover the dish with a dome of foil.

7. Bake in a preheated oven, 180°C/350°F/Gas Mark 4, for 30-40 minutes, or until the birds are completely cooked, turning them onto their other side halfway through the cooking time.

Cook's Notes

 Time
Preparation takes about 15 minutes, cooking takes about 40 minutes.

 Serving Idea
Serve with new potatoes, carrots and mange tout peas.

 Variation
If wished, substitute the saffron with turmeric, which will still give colour, but the flavour will not be the same.

SERVES 4

CHICKEN AND SHRIMPS WITH PASTA IN A CREAM SAUCE

The combination of chicken and seafood is always
a success when having guests for dinner.

460g/1lb boneless chicken breasts
90ml/6 tbsps white wine
Salt and freshly ground pepper
175g/6oz shelled broad beans (before removing
  outer skins)
60g/2oz potted shrimps
30g/1oz (scant) plain flour
280ml/½ pint single cream
1 heaped tbsp chopped fresh dill or 1 tsp dried dill
Cooked pasta, to serve

Step 1 Cut chicken breasts, across the grain, into 2cm/¾inch wide strips.

1. Cut the chicken breast into strips about 2cm/¾ inch wide, put them into a shallow ovenproof dish, pour over the wine and season with salt and pepper.

2. Cover and cook in a preheated oven for about 25 minutes at 180°C/350°F/Gas Mark 4, until tender. Allow to cool, then cut the strips in half lengthwise.

3. Strain and reserve the cooking liquid.

4. Cook the beans until just tender, then drain and remove the white outer skins. (If you use frozen broad beans the skins can be slipped off before cooking, as the beans have already been blanched.)

5. Melt the potted shrimps over a gentle heat then stir in the flour and blend carefully. Continue cooking for 1-2 minutes, stirring constantly.

6. Make the single cream up to 420ml/¾ pint using the reserved cooking liquid. Off the heat, stir this into the floured shrimps and return to a low heat, stirring until you have a smooth sauce.

7. Add the dill and the shelled beans and season to taste. Stir in the chicken strips, heat gently until warmed and serve with pasta.

Step 5 Stir the flour into the melted potted shrimps and blend carefully over a gentle heat.

Step 7 Stir in the chicken strips and heat gently to warm through.

Cook's Notes

Time
Preparation takes about 15 minutes and cooking takes about 30 minutes.

Variation
This recipe can be made with ready-cooked chicken.

Serving Idea
Serve with a green side salad. A chilled white Alsace wine always complements pasta.

SERVES 4

PECAN CHICKEN

Pecans can be used in both sweet and savoury dishes.
Here their rich, sweet taste complements a stuffing for chicken.

4 boned chicken breasts
45g/1½oz butter or margarine
1 small onion, finely chopped
90g/3oz pork sausage meat
90g/3oz fresh breadcrumbs
1 tsp chopped fresh thyme
1 tsp chopped fresh parsley
1 small egg, lightly beaten
120g/4oz pecan halves
280ml/½ pint chicken stock
1 tbsp flour
2 tbsps sherry
Salt and pepper
Chopped parsley or 1 bunch watercress to garnish

1. Cut a small pocket in the thick side of each chicken breast using a small knife.

2. Melt 15g/½oz of the butter in a small saucepan and add the onion. Cook a few minutes over gentle heat to soften. Add the sausage meat and turn up the heat to brown. Break up the sausage meat with a fork as it cooks.

3. Drain off excess fat and add the breadcrumbs, herbs and a pinch of salt and pepper to the pan. Allow to cool slightly and add enough egg to hold the mixture together. Chop pecans, reserving 8, and add to the stuffing.

4. Using a teaspoon, fill the pocket in each chicken breast with some of the stuffing.

5. Melt another 15g/½oz of the butter in a casserole and place in the chicken breasts, skin side down first. Brown over moderate heat and turn over. Brown the other side quickly to seal.

6. Pour in the stock, cover the casserole and cook for about 25-30 minutes in a preheated 180°C/350°F/ Gas Mark 4 oven until tender.

7. When chicken is cooked, remove it to a serving plate to keep warm. Reserve and strain the cooking liquid.

8. Melt remaining butter in a small saucepan and stir in the flour. Cook to a pale straw colour. Stir in the cooking liquid and add the sherry. Bring to the boil and stir constantly until thickened. Add the reserved pecans and seasoning.

9. Spoon some of the sauce over the chicken. Garnish with chopped parsley or a bunch of watercress.

Step 1 Use a small, sharp knife to cut a pocket in each chicken breast.

Step 4 Open each pocket in the chicken and spoon in the stuffing.

 *Cook's Notes*

 Time
Preparation takes about 30 minutes and cooking takes about 40 minutes

 Variation
If pecans are unavailable, use hazelnuts. Crush the hazelnuts roughly for the garnish and brown lightly in the butter before adding flour for the sauce.

Serving Idea
Serve with rice or sauté potatoes, broccoli and carrots.

SERVES 4-6

CHICKEN WITH AUBERGINE AND HAM STUFFING

Aubergines and ham make an unusual
stuffing and add interest to roast chicken.

1 small aubergine
30g/1oz butter or margarine
1 small onion, finely chopped
120g/4oz ham, chopped
120g/4oz fresh breadcrumbs
2 tsps chopped mixed herbs
1-2 eggs, beaten
Salt and pepper
1 x 1.4kg/3lb chicken
30g/1oz additional butter, softened

Step 1 Sprinkle the cut surface of the aubergine lightly with salt and leave to stand.

1. Cut the aubergine in half lengthways and remove stem. Lightly score the surface with a sharp knife and sprinkle with salt. Leave to stand for about 30 minutes for the salt to draw out any bitter juices.

2. Melt the butter in a medium saucepan and when foaming, add the onion. Cook slowly to soften slightly.

3. Rinse the aubergine and pat dry. Cut into 1.25cm/½ inch cubes. Cook with the onion until fairly soft. Add the remaining ingredients except the chicken and softened butter, beating in the egg gradually until the mixture just holds together. Add salt and pepper to taste.

4. Remove the fat from just inside the chicken cavity. Fill the neck end with the stuffing. Place any extra in a greased casserole. Tie the legs together place the chicken in a roasting tin. Spread over the softened butter and roast in a pre-heated 180°C/350°F/Gas Mark 4 oven for about 1 hour, or until the juices from the chicken run clear when the thickest part of the thigh is pierced with a sharp knife.

5. Cook extra stuffing, covered, for the last 35 minutes of cooking time. Leave the chicken to stand for 10 minutes before carving. If wished, make gravy with the pan juices.

Step 4 Remove the fat from just inside the cavity opening.

Cook's Notes

Time
Preparation takes about 30 minutes and cooking takes about 5-6 minutes for the stuffing and about 1 hour for the chicken.

Variation
Other ingredients, such as chopped red or green peppers, celery or spring onions, may be added to the stuffing.

Watchpoint
Do not stuff the chicken until ready to cook.

SERVES 4

CHICKEN THIGHS IN PERNOD

Your guests will feel extremely pampered
when they sit down to this dish.

30g/1oz butter
8 chicken thighs
2 shallots, finely chopped
2 tbsps water
75ml/5 tbsps Pernod
Salt and freshly ground black pepper

Step 1 Sauté the chicken for 8 minutes to brown on all sides.

1. Melt the butter in a large frying pan. When hot, sauté the thighs for 8 minutes, browning on all sides. Reduce the heat, add the shallots and water and cover the pan.

2. Continue to simmer for another 30-35 minutes, or until the chicken portions are cooked.

3. Remove the lid, increase the heat and pour in the Pernod.

4. Set alight with a match, shake the pan and turn off the heat. When the flames die down, scrape up any browned juices from the bottom of the pan.

5. Remove the chicken portions to a warm serving dish. Season the remaining juices with salt and pepper and bring to the boil. Spoon over the chicken and serve.

Step 3 Increase the heat and pour in the Pernod.

Step 4 Scrape up any browned meat juices from the bottom of the pan.

Cook's Notes

 Time
Preparation takes about 20 minutes and cooking takes about 30-35 minutes.

 Serving Idea
Serve on a bed of rice with a selection of seasonal vegetables.

 Variation
Add a little cream to the sauce just before serving, and heat through.

SERVES 4

POUSSINS ESPAGNOLE

The olive oil in this recipe gives
a wonderful flavour to the sauce.

4 single (small) poussins
Salt and fresh ground black pepper
Olive oil, to brush
4 small wedges of lime or lemon
4 bay leaves
2 tbsps olive oil
1 small onion, thinly sliced
1 clove garlic, crushed
460g/1lb tomatoes
140ml/¼ pint red wine
140ml/¼ pint chicken or vegetable stock
1 tbsp tomato purée
1 green chilli, seeded and thinly sliced
1 small red pepper, cut into thin strips
1 small green pepper, cut into thin strips
2 tbsps chopped, blanched almonds
1 tbsp pine nuts
12 small black olives, pitted
1 tbsp raisins

1. Rub the poussins inside and out with salt and pepper. Brush the skins with olive oil and push a wedge of lemon or lime, and a bay leaf into the cavity of each one.

2. Roast the poussins, uncovered, in a preheated oven 190°C/375°F/Gas Mark 5 for 45 minutes, or until just tender.

3. Meanwhile, heat the 2 tbsps olive oil in a large frying pan and gently cook the onion and the garlic until they are soft, but not coloured.

4. Cut a slit into the skins of each tomato and plunge into boiling water for 30 seconds.

5. Using a sharp knife carefully peel away the skins from the blanched tomatoes.

6. Chop the tomatoes roughly. Remove and discard the seeds and cores.

7. Add the chopped tomatoes to the cooked onion and garlic, and fry gently for a further 2 minute.

8. Add the remaining ingredients and simmer for 10-15 minutes, or until the tomatoes have completely softened and the sauce has thickened slightly.

9. Arrange the poussins on a serving dish and spoon a little of the sauce over each one.

10. Serve hot with the remaining sauce in a separate jug.

Step 3 Fry the onion and garlic gently in the olive oil until they are soft but not coloured.

Step 5 Using a sharp knife carefully peel away the loosened skins from the blanched tomatoes.

Cook's Notes

Time
Preparation takes 15 minutes, cooking takes about 1 hour.

Serving Idea
Serve with rice and a mixed green salad.

Cook's Tip
If the poussins start to get too brown during the cooking time, cover them with aluminium foil.